Call Me Madam

Call Me Madam

From Mother to Madam

DAWN ANNANDALE

First published in 2008 by Fusion Press,
a division of Satin Publications Ltd
101 Southwark Street
London SE1 0JF
UK
info@visionpaperbacks.co.uk
www.visionpaperbacks.co.uk
Publisher: Sheena Dewan

A catalogue record for this book is available from
the British Library.

ISBN: 978-1-905745-37-1

2 4 6 8 10 9 7 5 3 1

Cover design by Lee Motley
Text design by ok?design
Cover photo: Jason Langer/Getty Images
Initial Edit by Jeremy Thwaites
Printed and bound in the UK by
Cox and Wyman

Acknowledgements

Rebecca, I still have your umbrella. Don't use it much any more, but nice to know it's there. You are a star and I am, and always will be, eternally grateful.

Jeremy, thank you for your faith and for taking a chance on me. Much love. Mary, you always said I could do it – thank you for believing in me.

Kerry, Lois and Steve, Phil and Janine, John and Debbie, Graham, Tracy, Hannah and Simon, all of you will surely go to heaven. Anna and Michael Thwaites, two of the sweetest people I have ever had the good fortune to meet.

To all at Vision, Sheena, Kate, Tabitha, Louise, Anna and Paul. Grateful thanks for everything.

Dedication

For my children,
who are wonderful, most of the time.

Prologue

When I look back at my life over the years, I still have difficulty believing it all happened the way that it did. Here I stand, the mother of six children, all of whom have, in their own individual way, enriched my life and made it what it is. And yet there have been times when, if I am truthful, I just didn't know how I was going to meet the challenges life threw at me without going out of my mind.

I can remember vividly when my story – or rather, the more dramatic aspects of it – began. I was the ripe old age of 30, standing in my kitchen and staring into the open drawer that contained numerous unpaid bills: gas, electricity, phone, mortgage, water rates, council tax, TV licence – you name it, we hadn't paid it. This had been going on for months. That night, as I listened to the sound of my husband, Paul, snoring away in front of the blaring television, I knew finally that I had to do something.

1

There was a strong chance that he'd never hold down a proper job again because of health issues. And so, I made the extraordinary and, some would say, unimaginable decision to become an escort, or prostitute. It wasn't quite as cut and dried as that; a light bulb didn't appear over my head that instant, but rather the next day as I sat at work, flicking through the copy of *Ms London* I'd been handed that morning as I climbed up the steps of Chancery Lane tube station.

I had six children ranging in age from ten to just under a year. We lived in a lovely house in Kent, we had a car and, to the outside world, we were a normal, happy family. The truth was, of course, that we didn't have a penny to our names, and the bailiffs were threatening to take away whatever they could to cover the cost of one of many outstanding bills. I was working as a legal secretary in the City but no amount of overtime was making a dent on our outgoings – and, meanwhile, my husband, whom I still loved very much, wouldn't – indeed, couldn't – find a way out of our domestic crisis. And so, one morning, after scanning the ads, I made the call that would change my life forever. It was my decision alone. No one forced me so it was a choice that I have to live with. For the rest of my life, every time I set foot out of my front door, I know that virtually everyone I meet sees me, first and foremost, as that woman who went on the game. Only my closest friends see beneath the surface and, I hope, understand why I did what I did.

I worked as an escort for nearly three years. I saw everything in that time, mostly men who were so lonely they just wanted the chance to talk to a woman, face to face, about their lives, their hopes and their future. I also met monsters who treated me like filth and reminded me, again and again, that the sex industry is one of the most dangerous occupations in the world. Years later, I look back at that day, that hour, when I picked up the phone and made the call to the escort agency, and wonder how life would have panned out if I hadn't done it. A totally futile exercise because I can't go back in time; all I can do is live with my conscience and my decision. However, I strongly believe that what I did was right at the time. The life-altering decision hinged on security, stability and the love I felt for my children, coupled with an overwhelming feeling of responsibility, but we all have our limits, our breaking point, and I could only do it for so long.

I went on working, night after night, always thinking, 'Just a little bit longer, and then I can pack this in for good.' After nearly three years, I had managed to pay off our debts and secure some sort of future for myself and the children. By that time, my marriage was over and, though Paul still saw the children, he had moved out of the house.

I didn't really plan my so-called career break. The decision to stop working had come after a night that I thought would never end. I worked for an escort agency based in London that was run by a woman I hardly knew called Holly. She would phone me on the nights I was working and tell me where my first booking would take me. I'd been with Holly for a good couple of years and I'd proved to be reliable – most employers will tell you that working mothers make the best employees. The trouble was the travelling.

This agency's advertising covered such a huge area, from Oxford to Dover, Worthing to Milton Keynes. After six months of paying a driver for each evening, I had a core of regular clients and felt safe driving myself. But on some nights I could find myself on a marathon between Milton Keynes and Worthing via North London, with other stops along the M25 to fit in.

On the night in question, I had had what can only be described as one of the worst days of my life, which had started with a horrible, sickening fight with the man who really did mean more to me than anyone ever had – my boyfriend, David.

Holly called me mid-afternoon to let me know that my first booking would be at 8.00 pm with Ron, who lived near Dartford, which meant leaving home around 7.15 pm. I pushed the argument to the back of my mind and prepared to face the rest of the day. As usual, I cooked the supper and sat with the children as they ate, chatting about their school day. Emily talked about her singing teacher and how she was looking forward to an important competition at school; Alice made us all laugh at her impersonation of her geography teacher; Alexander was looking forward to Saturday's rugby match against a neighbouring school; Deborah, pony-mad, listened intently to the chatter, whilst little Victoria and my baby, Jack, played with their food and vied for my attention.

After making sure the children had all they needed, and checking once more to see that Jack was soundly asleep, I said goodbye to my trusted babysitter, and headed off into the night. I was wearing a smart, knee-length black dress, court shoes and

4

matching bag. My work clothes. The children and the babysitter, and everyone else bar a few, believed that I worked for a large and well-known group of solicitors in the City, providing night-time cover – the graveyard shift, as it was known.

As I drove through heavy traffic, humming along with Rod Stewart, Holly called me on my mobile to let me know that Anthony, another good client who lived in Tunbridge Wells, would also like to see me that evening. There would be more bookings as the night went on.

I rang Holly as I pulled up outside the house near Dartford and told her I would ring her once I'd left Ron. Sighing, resigned to the evening's work, the electric gates opened and I drove through them onto the gravel drive, entering that 'other' world. This was the moment when I abandoned my identity as Dawn and became, for the night, Elizabeth – a single mother working to put her only child, a boy, through private school. Ron treated me like a girlfriend and, as I walked into the house, he discreetly slipped an envelope containing my fee – £240 for a two-hour booking – into my coat pocket. Holly would receive £80 of that fee for having provided the booking service.

Ron was of pretty average build. He could perhaps have benefited from a little more exercise, but he was never less than charming, and he always smelt clean. The house was immaculate and he seemed completely at ease, probably because his wife and children were miles away, staying with her parents in the country for the weekend. Ron would join them the following day. As always, he chatted about his family, work, his mates at the cricket club and how he never wanted me to leave. Eventually, he slipped his hand into mine and gently pulled me to my feet. We went upstairs, I gently massaged his back, we had sex, and then, after a decent interval, I showered, kissed him goodbye and headed off into the night, promising to see him again very soon.

I called Holly to let her know I was on my way to see Anthony in Tunbridge Wells and I could hear her noting down the duration of that first booking. Sometimes it seemed like these were just a series of money-making exercises to her, one after the other. Sure enough, just as I was about to put down the phone, Holly told me that Dan in Reigate also wanted me tonight. He only ever booked me and so was happy to wait until I could get there. I told Holly I'd be with him at about 12.30 am, give or take. The logistics of my job were a nightmare. You never knew who wanted to see you on which night and whilst you might get lucky and land a couple of jobs in the same area, it was just as likely that they would be 50 miles apart. And so the night had begun.

I eventually arrived at Dan's after seeing Anthony and began another session of what he believed to be passionate and meaningful sex. In this business, you have to adopt a mindset and stick with it; it's a bit like being an actor. If you can't maintain the outward appearance of enjoying every minute, the chances are you won't get invited back again. Most of the escorts that I've known want to build up a list of regulars because then they are minimising the risk factor. Many of the clients like the familiarity too, because once they get to know you, they can relax and they are then able to be more open about their fantasies. When a man phones an escort agency, he won't usually ask, on the first booking, for anything specific, just the length of time he requires the girl to be with him. A lot of men book for two hours and then find they probably should have booked for 20 minutes! Once he's established that the girl is someone he can relax with, he will then ask her, often in a slightly embarrassed fashion, if the next time she sees him she might bring along a particular outfit or toy. It's all a case of careful negotiation.

As I lay in Dan's bed that night having sex, making sure he believed it was making love, I heard a text message being delivered to my phone. It was probably my one-hour warning from Holly. As we were reaching a somewhat critical point in the proceedings, I ignored the phone and concentrated on puffing and panting in the right places. After Dan had collapsed in a heap beside me, he stroked my hair and told me how much I meant to him and asked me why didn't I leave all this and marry him. Oh God, not again . . .

Thankfully, Holly's timing was for once spot-on and my phone started to ring. But, my relief at being saved from Dan's declarations of undying love soon turned to horror as I listened to Holly say that Sam back in Dartford wanted to see me. I was warm, cosy, sleepy and exhausted and could have cried. I agreed to have dinner with Dan later in the week to talk. On autopilot, I showered, dressed, sorted out my make-up and kissed him goodbye on the cheek. He watched me, the sadness in his eyes almost tangible and I couldn't bear to look at him. I didn't get to Sam until about 3.00 am. I wearily got through this last job and then I was finally in the car and on my way home. I started the engine and headed out to the motorway listening to Charlie Wolf on 'TalkSport' chatting to some nutcase who wanted to save the world from the green lizards that were overtaking us. Great, just me and the lunatics, I thought. I was so tired. 'You're nearly home,' I heard myself say. 'Yes, not far at all: M25, M2 – you're almost there.' The sounds of the radio dissolved into mindless chatter. I remember hearing Charlie Wolf laugh, and then I absorbed the darkness of the night sky, the monotony of the road . . . the world went black.

I came to and slowly realised what had happened. I had fallen asleep and hit the central reservation. I wasn't dead, but I was scared out of my wits. The car engine had stalled. What if I hadn't been wearing my seat belt? What if I'd driven into another car? I felt sick and cold with the fear and loneliness of it all. I restarted the engine and gently eased the car over to the hard shoulder, unable to believe just how lucky I had been. What if another car had been behind me? What if . . . ? But I was alive, and now I knew this *had* to be the end. The cup of coffee I had bought hours ago was stone cold, but I was so dehydrated with fear that it would have to do.

I pulled myself together and slowly drove to the nearest petrol station, awake for England on all the adrenalin flooding through my body, and walked shakily inside to buy another coffee. Back in the warm and familiar surroundings of my car, I knew I couldn't possibly go on with this any longer. I reached for my mobile and made the call, the smell of the coffee pervading the car interior. 'Enough is enough, Holly; a million pounds won't make me do this any more.' I told her I was going home to my children and would never work for the agency again. I didn't wait for her response, I just cut the call and turned my phone off. It really didn't matter any more. This was my end, my breaking point, and suddenly I knew I had to get my life back into perspective. I drove home, slowly and very carefully. For the first time in as long as I could remember, I felt genuinely happy.

The next morning I woke up feeling as though today was the first day of the rest of my life, as the saying goes. Of course there was so much to be resolved, not just financially, but in every area of my life. At the front of my mind, of course, was my partner David, the man who had taken my breath away, who had saved me from utter despair when my marriage to Paul had come crashing down around me. I had got to know David when I was working as a legal secretary in the City. We'd known each other to wave to on an almost daily basis for years, as he lived across the street from me. Gradually, we began to commute together, and David became my confidant more than anything. As things with Paul got worse, David and I became romantically involved, and when we both ended the already doomed relationships with our respective partners we officially became an item.

Just a few hours before I'd begun work that night, David had confronted me with the evidence I had so hoped he would never obtain. A chance remark by a friend, a call to a private detective and David had discovered my secret, the one thing I hoped he'd never find out about me: that the woman he thought he knew and loved was not a part-time legal secretary, working nights in the City, but a prostitute – a whore, a tart, a hooker. I might try to comfort myself with the belief that I was a high-class, sophisticated escort with a small and carefully selected list of clients, but the fact was that I was being paid to have sex night after night with strangers. And, unsurprisingly, David's world imploded. He was hurt beyond measure – I had lied to him, deceived him, and he couldn't deal with it. He had visited me earlier that day and, after loveless sex, had thrown a cheque on the bed for services rendered, before crashing out of my front door and, as far as I knew, out of my life forever. I used to say, 'Call me Elizabeth,' to my clients. And that's just what he did, in mockery of my working name.

In the early morning light, as I stirred my tea and wondered if I'd made the right decision to stop working, a flash of something caught my eye. I looked out of the window and there he was, smiling at me: David. As he came into the kitchen, his arms held open in an embrace, I sensed that we might have a second chance. This good man – so earnest, so quiet – was about to forgive me. It would take months before he would learn to trust me again, but as we stood together in the kitchen, with him asking me, over and over again, why I hadn't confided in him, I knew that we had a chance. David stepped back and looked me squarely in the eye. I met his gaze. 'We'll talk later. Okay? I've got to go to work but I'll see you this evening, after the kids are in bed,' he said. He smiled and then turned and disappeared to his car, off to his job of computers, normality and predictability.

I heard noises upstairs, movement, and Scooby, our excitable black Labrador, barking. The children were waking up, completely unaware of the drama which had unfolded one floor beneath them. I immediately slipped into mummy mode and thought about Sugar Puffs and boiled eggs. I savoured every moment as I helped the children to get ready for school that morning. We were a large family, what with my six children, me and Scooby. Ever since I had been small all I had ever truly wanted was loads of kids – loads of noisy, happy, naughty children to fill that ache, that huge gaping hole in my heart which should have been filled with love and security from my parents. I walked up the stairs, happy, smiling to myself, ready to change my life. As the kids ate breakfast, found ties, hats, jumpers, homework, cleaned their teeth and eventually piled into the car ready to go to school, I felt elated. For so long I had come in from the night's work completely exhausted and longing for my bed, never knowing when it would end, never even thinking about the end, only the need to continue, to provide.

I dropped the kids at school and came home to the usual routine of shoving washing in the machine, loading the dishwasher and remembering to take mince out of the freezer for dinner. Scooby needed his breakfast as well as a quick walk, so I collected his lead and had a wander in the woods at the back of the house, exhausted, my eyes prickling and stinging. When Scooby and I returned home, I collapsed into bed for a few hours. Even though I slept for about four hours, I felt overwhelmed with a multitude of emotions. I was desperately tired, but not in the usual exhausted lack-of-sleep way; this was tired of my old life, tired from the worry, deceit and the trepidation I felt every time I knocked on a new client's door. But that tiredness was smouldering away in a cauldron of hope for the future, coupled with a sense of relief. The sheer relief that I was not going to drive hundreds of miles around the country any more; relief that tonight I would get to put my children to bed and then stay at home with the ironing and *EastEnders* for company. I picked the kids up from school and went through the usual nightly rigmarole of homework, squabbles, forgotten lunch boxes and lost jumpers. We finally sat down to supper at about 6.30 pm and, as I dished up the spaghetti, I told the children I had some news for them. I said I had decided to change my job and had handed my notice in but, as I had some holiday owing, I didn't have to go into work any more. Obviously I would eventually have to find another job but not for a few months at least. As they munched on their garlic bread they asked a few questions and I reassured them that, yes, everything was fine and, yes, I was going to be at home with them full-time for a little while. Alexander said that Louise, their babysitter, let them stay up much later than I did, so would I kindly retract my notice please? Alexander's silly request, coupled with the absence of follow-up questions reassured me that the kids felt secure and comfortable with these changes.

Over the next few weeks, David and I talked, and it was not always smooth sailing. He just couldn't understand why I hadn't told him the truth about what I was doing. Hindsight is a marvellous thing, and we would all do things so differently with the benefit of it. If I had known David then the way I know him now then, yes, I would have told him the truth from the start and saved us both a great deal of heartache. So, I told him everything – from the weird situations, to the lonely people, the miles and miles of driving, the mountains of debt, the visits from the bailiffs and Paul's unwillingness to take his head out of the sand. He was amazed, saying that he never had an inkling of what was going on. That's so true, isn't it? We really don't know what does go on behind closed doors. Outwardly, Paul and I, with our children and nice house, appeared to be one big happy family, but peel away a few layers, and look what you reveal; debt, arguments and deep unhappiness.

David began to understand my exhaustion, my sadness, and when he gently coaxed from me the traumas of my childhood, he began to understand slowly my deep-rooted need, my passion even, to provide for and be all-encompassing for my children. I know that forgiving and forgetting are two very separate emotions, but for now we closed the door on the past.

Chapter One

When I met my husband, Paul, it was as though I had finally found my soulmate. My teenage years had been, to say the least, a bit reckless, but now I was determined to put the past behind me and become the kind of mother to my own children that I had never had. At just 24, I already had Emily and Alice to care for; Paul took my precious girls to his heart and they in turn loved him as if he were their father.

Once married, we quickly started to build our family and by the time we'd been together for six years, Alexander, Deborah, Victoria and Jack had all been born. Six children and, to tell the truth, I might have gone on to have more were it not for the fact that reality began to bite and the bills started stacking up. I take full responsibility for my part in our troubles and there's no doubt that if I'd had a more ordinary view of what makes a happy family, things might have turned out differently.

In the end, I worked for nearly three years as an escort and managed to pay off our debts. The house I saved; the marriage I couldn't. After long discussions, we decided it would be for the best if we started divorce proceedings.

Being a single parent is a thankless task. Namely because the logistics of the job seem to require you to be in two places at once. Then there's the baggage that inevitably accompanies you. I think the first emotion I felt when my marriage broke down was anger, then bitterness. But in time, once the sting has subsided, the guilt overtakes it with a passion. I still feel so guilty about having failed to stay with Paul, having failed in my marriage vows, having failed to give my children that security of having their mum and dad together. It's all so sad – such a waste of dreams and love – but our relationship was over, and we had both accepted that fact. I consulted a solicitor and started the ball rolling. Thankfully, the one thing that so often turns divorce into full-scale war was not an issue: Paul had no intention of contesting custody of the children.

My greatest fear of course was that he would discover I had been working as an escort. His parents knew my secret – they'd had their suspicions for months and a private detective had confirmed them. I couldn't believe it. I had been followed, my movements noted, and then the inevitable confrontation by phone from Paul's mother, Jan, all just weeks before I was to stop. Naturally I was terrified they would tell him. In fact, Jan had no intention of doing any such thing. I think she knew it would break his heart, so her loyalty to her son ultimately protected me. Paul moved out of our house about a year before I gave up work and he was living with his mother and step-father when we started the divorce proceedings. Although the children went to the house to see him, he knew that, because I felt he was drinking a fair bit at the time, I wouldn't let him have the kids unsupervised. The children saw him when he was with his mum and step-dad.

The divorce went through pretty quickly with minimum cost and disruption. We agreed to sell the house and I made an undertaking that Paul would get a reasonable share of the fairly slim equity to put down on a house for himself, as and when he was ready to live on his own. And that was it. Eleven years of my life over in a matter of days. We had married and had four beautiful children together and now all that love was about to be reduced to a piece of paper: Decree Absolute. It was the exact opposite of the perfect family I had dreamt of. Now all I had to look forward to was joining the set of 'every-other-weekend' families, full of complications and awkwardness at weddings, parents' evenings and graduations. I thought about our wedding, itself a major exercise in diplomacy. With my family so estranged from me, and Paul's parents divorced, the business of putting together a workable seating plan nearly did it for me! And that was before we'd even organised the photos and briefed the photographer to call Paul's mum by her new surname.

As much as I wanted to protect the kids from the harsh realities of life, I obviously had to tell them that their dad and I were getting divorced. More often than not, the news that their parents are getting divorced doesn't get much of a reaction from the children – the slow breakdown of the marriage separation has already caused the upset. I remember the knots I had in my stomach when I tried to find the words to explain to the kids that Paul and I had actually split up – that daddy had moved out for good. Deborah, at the tender age of seven, just shrugged when I told her, as though I was keeping her up to date with the plot line of *Neighbours*. Of course, her flippant gesture had never been meant like that, but what else could she say? After all, even at that age, probably still harbouring a dream of reunion, she knew that nothing she did or said was likely to change our minds.

No, the hard emotional battle had already been endured when Paul moved out and the kids had, as far as I could tell, adjusted to that. Not happily by any means, of course; we all would much rather have been the happy family unit we once were, but that was never going to happen so we had to try to move on. They knew that Daddy lived with Grandma and Grandad, and that they could always go and see him there.

We had lived in our house for about five years and, although I was sad to be selling up after all it had taken to keep it from being repossessed, I felt that the children had adjusted well to Paul's departure the year before, and could now cope with moving house. I still think about that house to this day – my dream home. It was lovely; backing onto the woods, it had lots of open space inside and that warm familiarity you get from the home where you've raised your babies. I needed to come up with something reassuring, so I explained to the children that we would find a house much nearer to all their friends from school. To

Emily and Alice, being that much older, I also explained that, as Paul and I were getting divorced, he was entitled to some money from the sale, so I had to sell up and move on.

The house went on the market in the autumn and, newly liberated from working the night, I spent virtually every waking moment trying to find us somewhere to live. Of course, with no monthly income, I knew I'd have to rent somewhere until I'd managed to come up with something more solid. What that was to be, I didn't know.

The hunt was now on for somewhere big enough and affordable, closer to school and available soon. On the one hand, I was loath to leave this house, which I had worked so hard to keep, but on the other, it was also a form of release because it was the one thing that tied me legally to Paul and now that tie would be severed. The children had adjusted well, in time, to the fact that they had joined the ranks of the so-called broken family. In a cruel way, the mere fact that there are so many divorces almost helps, because they all had friends who had already been through the process and survived. I now worried about the kids adjusting to a new home but, thankfully, they were all excited and were treating it as one big adventure. It was one thing they had to get used to at a time in their lives when all else was happiness and contentment so, if there ever is a right time, I felt that it was then.

I called the estate agent and before long we had a buyer, the contents of the house were in boxes and being loaded onto a removal van, and another step was being taken away from the past, towards a brand new future.

The town house I found to rent was in Rochester. It was virtually brand new and, with four bedrooms, it would certainly do as a stopgap for me and the children, though the lack of a proper garden was going to prove to be a bit of a challenge, especially with a lively Labrador to think of! Still, the park across the road compensated for that. I took the children to see the house before we moved in and explained that I knew it wasn't quite as big as our last home, but we would only live in it for a year at the most whilst we looked for a lovely big house to buy, with a big garden and a bedroom each. I heard myself promising the earth and wondered how I was possibly going to pay the rent on this house, let alone afford a mortgage on a house with a bedroom each.

We finally moved three weeks before Christmas. I was no longer Paul's wife, nor was I a name on a roster of escorts; I was just me again and, coupled with the sale of the house, I felt free. The two oldest girls, Emily and Alice, shared a bedroom on the ground floor. They seemed to adjust to the move quite quickly, and Emily especially liked the fact that her best friend lived around the corner and that they could walk to school together. Alexander and Jack crammed into one of the bedrooms upstairs, Jack loving the chance to share with his big brother at last, big brother not quite sharing his enthusiasm. And for now, Deborah grumpily tolerated the intrusion of Victoria, jealously guarding her My Little Pony collection from her younger sister. It didn't take long for them all to start treating the nearby park as their back garden. My room was my sanctuary. 'Very cosy' is how I think an estate agent would describe it! Of course, in spite of all my fears about the children suffering from the disruption, the whole experience was very exciting and my worries were fast dispelled.

There were many changes, but one thing I was simply not prepared to do at this point was take the children out of their independent school and move them into the nearby state primary. I've taken a lot of criticism for this over the years, and if the local state school hadn't been so dismal, I would happily have moved them. The classes there were jam-packed, and the teachers overwhelmed with social problems which they were expected to deal with, on top of trying to educate the children. I just couldn't do it. The children had already undergone enough disruption for now and, in my humble opinion, children are not as adaptable as we like to think.

The extra half hour in bed each morning was a lovely bonus for us all, as the house was so much closer to school, and Emily, who went to the local girls' grammar school, now walked there instead of enduring a long bus ride. It's the little things that contributed to a feeling of safety and peace. David stayed over frequently, and little by little we were mending our relationship. Paul saw the children from time to time, they were all doing well at school and I felt as if I'd taken a huge step forward in sorting out my life in general. But there was a whole marathon ahead of me.

Summarising the situation in my mind, trying to take a few steps forward, the reality of my life was inescapable. I had left my husband and started divorce proceedings, given up my lucrative career as a highly paid escort, and now I was going to be a mum living off the money I had saved and the proceeds from the sale of the house. But then what? What would I do when the money ran out? So, as I cooked, cleaned, shopped, washed, ironed, taxied kids to and fro and recovered from the exhaustion of three years' nocturnal activity, I planned.

I turned over and over in my mind all the possibilities and weighed up where I was now. I started to think about opening my own escort agency, which until now had been nothing more than an idle dream. The agency I had worked for was lacking in the areas of security and safety, and the huge distances I was travelling in the course of one night had caused numerous problems. It was only because I was in so much debt and so desperate that I tolerated the logistical nightmare that was my working week. However, the legal implications of running my own escort agency, the moral dilemma of making bookings for, and taking money from women who were having sex with men for cash, as well as the fact that I was still so physically exhausted, made me put the idea to one side. Instead, I began to look for an office job. I'd had a couple of permanent jobs in the past but really preferred to take on short-term contracts or work as a 'temp' where there was greater flexibility for arranging life around the kids.

With Christmas fast approaching, I decided to make the leap, so I phoned Simon, a recruitment consultant who'd got me many secretarial bookings over the years, and arranged to see someone in London the following week. He had looked after me well when I had worked in London as a temp. I told him I wanted a job within walking distance of Cannon Street Station, a float position

21

and as much money as possible. 'You haven't changed!' he laughed, and agreed to help me. Simon arranged a few interviews and eventually I accepted a position at a firm of solicitors in Blackfriars. The job was straightforward and I knew it inside out. The location was really convenient for Cannon Street and the money was enough to keep the wolf from the door, but I'd be taking home in a month less than I used to earn in a week, which was a bit of a shock. The following Monday morning I joined the commuters at Chatham Station and became a legal secretary once more. Now the children were that little bit older, childcare was not such a problem. There was a great after-school club, and when they weren't staying for an activity they went to the homework club. I had a friend whose husband was a taxi driver so he collected the kids for me from school each night and dropped them back home at about 6.00 pm. We all quickly and fairly effortlessly fell into a routine, which was helped by me buying a slow cooker so the evening meal was ready when I got in, and resigning myself to catching up with the housework as and when.

The normality of going to work in an office in London again was almost surreal in its mundanity. Every morning I rushed the kids out of bed to wash, dress, eat breakfast, sort out school bags, rugby kits, hockey sticks, homework – you know the drill. I dropped them off at school then caught the 8.28 am to Cannon Street, followed by the short walk down to Blackfriars and into work for 9.30. I worked at a huge firm of solicitors, so I was just an anonymous cog in the wheel of endless letters, faxes and emails – and I loved it. I simply loved the boring easiness of it.

Not having to think too hard about anything other than wading through the pile of audio tapes on my desk, filing paperwork or photocopying documents. There was nothing important or earth shattering, and it was heaven. Every lunchtime David would come and meet me as he worked ten minutes away. We would sit in the sun, eating our sandwiches on the steps of St Paul's Cathedral. God knows how many times a smiling tourist would ask us in broken English to take their photo in front this magnificent building that was my lunchtime retreat. I didn't earn very much – certainly not enough to cover all my outgoings – but what I did earn certainly slowed down the rate at which my savings were disappearing. So I typed and was happy, but one chance meeting changed all that in an instant.

'Elizabeth, my God! Hello!'

It was Monday morning and I was about two minutes away from walking into the office.

'Elizabeth!'

I hadn't been called that for some time now and the sound of the name brought an instant heady sickness with it. Two worlds were colliding – my past and my present had crashed into each other and I needed to run away as fast as I could. The man looking at me, smiling bemusedly, was Gareth Roberts, a man I'd had sex with on many occasions. Gareth was single, very attractive and very eligible. I had visited him at his home about twice a month for around a year and the visits always followed the same pattern. We would discuss whatever we'd been reading, films and exhibitions we'd seen, talk about politics or other world events.

Then he would invite me to go upstairs and prepare myself for him. Gareth was very straightforward in his requirements and the sex never lasted more than about 20 minutes. He liked white underwear and I always kept my high heels on for him. So, an hour or so after arriving, I would leave £150 richer and with Gareth's recommendation of a good book or film, which we would no doubt dissect on my next visit.

But here we were, 9.30 on a bright sunny morning in the heart of the City, both with our clothes on for a change. He was so pleased to see me and insisted on arranging a date for lunch. I agreed, just to get rid of him, because I was now late for work. Also, he had just told me where he worked and what he did: Gareth Roberts was the HR director where I worked.

We met a couple of days later in a nearby pub and he was determined to hear all about the real me. By now, Gareth knew my real name and admitted to having had a look at my personnel file. I think we were both struck by the ludicrous coincidence of the situation and he was definitely surprised to find that someone like me – his words – would have ventured into the seedy world of prostitution. People in general, and Gareth to a lesser degree, despite having first-hand experience, stereotyped prostitutes as creatures who frequent King's Cross – all leopard print and red lipstick. In fact, we met several more times for lunch and Gareth wanted to know the how and the why of it. I suppose as a personnel director he was naturally interested in people and what made them tick, but maybe, my cynical side told me, he was just worried that I might reveal our previous connection. When I realised he was even more concerned about this than me, I told him directly I was not about to divulge anything to anyone. The relief was visible.

The encounter with Gareth made me realise how small the world is. This conclusion was further reinforced one evening after work when I had gone for a drink with some girlfriends. There were four of us sitting at a table in an Italian wine bar when a waiter bought over a bottle of champagne. When we protested that we hadn't ordered it, he pointed to a couple of men sitting across the bar, one of whom I recognised immediately, though to this day I still can't remember his name. He sat there, smugly waving to us, and, like I had when I first saw Gareth, I felt sick, thinking, hell no, not another one. I told the girls it was a smarmy guy from work who had been coming on to me and added this lie to all the others that ate away at me, haunted me every day. I had to get away from my past. I knew it was only a matter of time before someone embarrassed me in front of my friends or, far worse, my children.

I'd never really planned to stay in my job longer than was absolutely necessary but I was going to have to stick it out until we'd at least found a house to buy. I'd been there for about eight months by then and the school holidays had been a logistical nightmare. The children had eight weeks of summer holiday and for two of those weeks they went to Cornwall with their father and grandparents. I took two weeks' holiday from work and we had a trip to Center Parcs. For the remainder I relied on friends, the holiday club at school and the local leisure centre play scheme. There are facilities available but you need a degree in computing and statistics at the very least to be able to manage the timetabling when you're 40 miles away from your many kids, whilst trying to do the job you are paid for!

So, without further ado, I stepped up my hunt for a long-term solution. At the top of my list was a house of our own – one which fulfilled the promises I had made to the kids. With my monthly salary coming in, I was in a position to apply for a mortgage. Eventually I found what I was looking for. The house was in Strood, had six bedrooms and a garden. So, I signed along the dotted line and took another small step. We moved into our new home in September and I had never felt happier.

The house needed a great deal doing to it but thankfully there was nothing wrong structurally. The kids rushed around picking out their bedrooms and exploring their new home. It was a house with great potential, set over three floors. My bedroom was on the top floor, which I guess had once been the servants' quarters, and had a tatty en-suite bathroom that I had grand plans for. There was a half-landing and a smaller room off that on the right which would be Jack's bedroom. And then you were on the first floor, where there were a further four bedrooms and a bathroom. On the ground floor was a lounge, leading into a conservatory that was the length of the house, a tiny spare room off that, and a large kitchen complete with beautiful old wood burner and room for a dining table. I wandered around the house, imagining how I would decorate each room – the colours, the curtains, the furniture, everything feeling so exciting and fresh.

The survey on the house had proved that it was sound but as I walked around the empty shell, trying to imagine how it would be in the future, I worried so much about the expense of it all and the enormous job I had undertaken in buying this house. Sure, it had fantastic potential but, as I didn't have a very large deposit, it was only just affordable. This was my house and mine alone, and that thought scared the life out of me. I suppose many people have stood in my shoes, divorcing and moving to a house which is their sole responsibility, from the joy of ownership to the burden of the mortgage. I thought about my promises to the kids, of having a lovely big garden and a bedroom each. Victoria and Deborah had to share a massive room, so I didn't quite make good on the promise, but they didn't seem to mind too much. Still, I worried that it would take forever, as well as a bottomless pit of money, to renovate the house. But that wasn't really what was important. What was important was that we had finally done it – we had moved to a house which we would slowly make our own, and could start afresh with our new life.

I had set aside a small amount of money for renovations and the work was progressing well. It had all been done as economically as possible, just emulsion on the walls and new bedroom carpets. Luckily the original floorboards downstairs were in fairly good repair and after being sanded and waxed they looked beautiful. The house was typically Edwardian – very high ceilings, original picture and dado rails, and a traditional pantry. A friend of mine's father was doing most of the work and the house was looking better all the time. Behind a chipboard panel in the lounge we had found a fireplace. After the most enormous amount of hard work the fireplace emerged with a beautiful set of original tiles on a marble plinth. By the time I had finished blackening the grate and the iron surround, and picking out the delicate raised pattern in gold leaf, it looked absolutely stunning.

I was still working but it was becoming increasingly clear to me that I simply could not manage a full-time job in the City and the many needs of my children. I started to plan my next steps as something would have to give sooner or later.

Chapter Two

Ever since we'd moved to our lovely new house, I knew that being perfectly realistic, my days as a legal secretary were numbered. I sat down and got out the calculator. I knew and had known for ages, if truth be told, that no secretarial job, however hard I worked, was going to keep me ahead of the endless round of family expenses. But there was simply no way that I could go back to escorting. I'd done it before and though I didn't have regrets I just couldn't – wouldn't – go back. I also wanted and needed to be at home with the children. It was then that I began seriously thinking through the possibility of running my own agency.

Working for Holly had taught me a lot about the business. In particular, it made me realise that there are a lot of women out there, like me, who have to work to keep their families together and the bills paid. The more I thought about it, and confided in a couple of close friends who knew all about my past, the more I was sure I could run things the way I wish they'd been run when

I was working. I know all about the moral arguments but it doesn't alter the fact that as long as men are willing to pay for sex, there will be escort agencies and prostitutes. For thousands of girls, this means entering into one of the most dangerous and deadly professions in the world where there are no rules, no limits and no safety nets. And the women who are often most attracted to prostitution are, by definition, almost always vulnerable and often desperate. Women like me. I was lucky – and when I say lucky, I don't mean that I avoided the perverts, the creeps and the misogynists. Far from it. But I did manage to retain my sanity and, most importantly, my life. And you can earn a lot of money by going on the game. But prostitution is a lonely business. The girls don't usually meet or talk to each other as most agencies keep the girls apart. They don't want them meeting up and sharing secrets, just in case they get ideas and start short-changing the agency or the madam.

But there is another way, and I was determined to see if I could run the kind of agency that I would have wanted to have worked for when I first started out – somewhere safe, which put the interests of the girls first. I can't pretend I was doing this for purely altruistic reasons. I am not Mother Teresa. But this was a business I knew. And if I could make it work without compromising myself or others, and make a living from it that would allow me to keep my family together and to keep them healthy, then I wasn't going to walk away from that chance. Not a decision that many will applaud – not even one that I was sure was right. As is so often the case, I acted first and thought later. And, as it would turn out, I was about to enter a world that, in spite of everything I had already seen, would turn out to be far more complex and murky than I could possibly have anticipated.

Call Me Madam

When I began to think through the logistics of setting up my own agency, I wasn't worried so much about the legality of it or the possibility that I would be accused of feeding on the weak and the vulnerable, as I was about making sure that I worked with women who knew exactly what they were doing and why. I needed to attract girls who were reliable, drug-free and confident enough to cope with the job. The first thing I had to do was to advertise. I knew I would be contacted by a lot of very desperate girls, girls who were supporting violent partners, drug habits or both. I couldn't help these girls. Their lives were so complicated – they would not want me telling them what to do or how to dress. They'd probably laugh at me and think me absurdly pretentious. The hard truth was that the kind of clients I knew I wanted to attract would not want these girls either. They were looking for substitute girlfriends, for women who would listen to them, who would make them feel special. Of course, in time, I would get my fair share of customers whom I wish we'd been able to avoid. But for now anyway, I had high ambitions.

All through the autumn, I continued to work as a legal secretary during the day whilst dedicating time in the evening to worrying away at my secret plan. I spent hours on the phone to my trusted girlfriends and started planning my timetable.

Meeting other women to discuss escorting as a career path is, without question, the weirdest thing I've done and, believe me, I've found myself in some pretty odd situations! One of the very first people I got to know was a lady called Christina who was as about as far removed from the conventional image of an escort as it's possible to imagine. When you think of escorts, you probably imagine either Julia Roberts – all long legs, slightly disorganised, gorgeous and sexy – or someone like Charlotte Rampling –

sophisticated, erotic and domineering. Christina looked more like my old headmistress, and frankly I was a bit scared of her.

I had recently joined a gym, nothing special, just a place to go and have a swim and chill out in the rare moments when the children were all spoken for on the weekend or after school. It was packed with reed-thin girls, all of whom seemed to delight in showing off their toned and buffed bodies, shining with the latest St Tropez tans, and with perfect legs tapering to beautifully pedicured feet. I, for my part, spent most of my time submerged in the pool, hoping that no one was watching when I clambered up the steps and into my robe before anyone caught a glimpse of the tell-tale cellulite and signs that I'd had a baby – or six.

It was so peaceful at the gym. Home was so noisy, work was noisy and even the journey to and from work was noisy. I craved that half an hour or so of quiet time, just swimming up and down the pool, in a world of my own – thinking, planning and having the luxury of the 30 minutes of pure tranquillity. It's the same story that many working mums have: the phone is constantly ringing, your boss is saying you're getting behind, the kids are all babbling at once, the telly *and* the radio are on, and there's different music blaring from several rooms in the house, and you just want to scream out 'Shut up!' But of course you don't. Instead you find a way of escaping and retaining your sanity, and swimming amongst the sylph-like waifs was my haven. Actually, there was hardly anyone else there, and sometimes I even had the whole pool to myself. I usually sat in the steam room for ten minutes after my swim and finished off in the Jacuzzi. It was there that I met Christina. We seemed to be on the same schedule, having dealt with the kids at home and coming out for an hour's peace before the next set of tasks called.

Christina lived with her partner, Gerry, not far from us. She had two children from her first marriage – a girl and a boy, who were seven and nine. We often sat in the Jacuzzi and chatted about kids, partners and life in general. Both she and Gerry had been made redundant about six months ago from very well-paid jobs at a large insurance company in the City. It had come as quite a blow for them to find themselves out of work, especially for Gerry, who was the wrong side of 50. Like so many couples in their situation, they were financing two sets of children, a big house, huge mortgage repayments, a leased car, credit-card repayments and several other pretty weighty financial commitments. It's what happens when you think you're in a well-paid job for life. Christina said she only went to the gym because she'd paid for the full year's membership just before she lost her job. She told me how they'd both been trying to find work and how soul-destroying it was. Christina was posh, very Cheltenham Ladies' College and cucumber sandwiches. I sensed that she felt she was letting everyone down on top of the financial pressures they were obviously under.

As time went by we talked more, and I finally summoned up the courage to tell her what I used to do for a living as well as my plans to open an escort agency. Far from being shocked, she opened up and told me how she and Gerry were into wife-swapping and swinging. Now it was my turn to be shocked! I could not believe that behind the jolly-hockey-sticks image lay such an unlikely secret. She had me in stitches over some of the stories she told and we soon became good friends, meeting for a drink some Saturday nights and lunch at each other's houses when I had a day off. Our friendship developed over several weeks and it soon became clear to me that Christina was really worried about her future, particularly how she and Gerry were going to keep up their mortgage repayments as well as pay all the other bills. It didn't occur to me at first that she might seriously be considering working as an escort until she came right out with it one morning and tentatively asked if women her age ever worked in the business.

'Of course they do!' I laughed. It didn't actually dawn on me that she was asking for herself. But she soon made it clear that not only was it something she was very serious about but that, oddly, she found it almost titillating. Now I was really worried. Was her partner behind this – was it some sort of weird game? It wouldn't be the first time a woman had been coerced by her husband or boyfriend to have sex with strangers for their pleasure. I asked her straight away if she'd discussed it with Gerry. She admitted that they'd been discussing nothing else for the past week. They were very comfortable and secure in their relationship; I suppose they must have been, to be able to get involved in wife-swapping the way they did. It was quite obvious that she was fully in charge of her destiny. Christina was nothing if not businesslike in her approach and, as we sat together one day in the Jacuzzi, she got me to explain precisely how the business worked, the kind of men that rang for escorts, and how much she could expect to make in a week.

I explained the financial side of the business as clearly as I could, emphasising that it was easy to find yourself in a cycle of working long hours, night after night, until you no longer really knew who you were. As we chatted, I realised how much I needed to talk about all of this, to get it off my chest, even now. In all the years I worked for Holly, I'd hardly ever met any of the other girls, and those I had encountered really did fit the stereotypical image of a prostitute. Christina, on the other hand, was so far at the other end of the spectrum that it was almost funny. She was around 5' 4", a size 16, quite attractive but, to be truthful, a little past her best. In her mind, she didn't look too bad for her 40 years and, to her credit, she could see no reason why any man wouldn't be thrilled to have her next to him in bed. Not only was Christina terribly confident, she was also one of the most organised people I've ever met. Her household was run like a military operation. She was quite helpful in many ways and when I took the first major step in my new career path, designating the little box room downstairs as an office, she came over to my house to let the telephone engineer in whilst I was at work. Whilst she was there she even put the new curtains up for me. I didn't feel intimidated by her, that's too strong a word; it was more like watching her do her thing, with just a hint of amusement. Even her lunch invitations sounded like instructions, and unless there was something else really important I just went with the flow. Christina was extremely efficient, had lots of very helpful suggestions and a fantastic memory for detail. She had so many good qualities but occasionally came across strongly because of her very forthright manner. She could always be relied upon in a crisis, was very logical and objective and, beneath all her bluster, was a loving and kind person.

Christina's decision to become a prostitute is one that I still think to this day she might have taken too lightly, which made me determined that she understood exactly what she was getting herself into. When I started on the game, my first encounter with this other world was a ten-minute interview with 'Jimmy the pimp' in a council house somewhere in north-west London. He wasn't threatening or scary, but he was running a business and he didn't want to hire girls who thought that all they were going to have to do for their money was hold hands. I vividly remember him looking quizzically at me as I stood in front of him in my work clothes, probably looking about as switched on as a 20-watt light bulb.

'You do realise, don't you, that you have to fuck them?' he said helpfully.

'Oh yes, yes of course.' God, he must have thought I was thick. But the fact was, until he uttered those immortal words, I don't think I had really thought it through.

I wasn't quite so blunt with Christina but I did sit her down and go through what I considered to be the golden rules. Rules that I would hear myself repeating time and again until they became as familiar as the days of the week. I had worked for Holly long enough to know that as much as she appeared to seem caring, all she'd really been interested in was her booking fee. Yes, of course I wanted to make a living, but it was never worth another woman taking stupid risks in an already dangerous industry for the sake of my measly £40. I thought about the rules that I would implement and rigidly stick to, how I would carefully vet the clients, as well as explain to the escorts how to look after themselves, and the precautions they needed to strictly adhere to. I'd received such invaluable advice when I had first started escort work. Advice, strangely enough, from two regulars, one who happened to be a doctor and the other a security expert, and at the time they were words of wisdom, heaven-sent.

The doctor had told me to ensure that I always used polyurethane condoms because they were so tough. He explained how easy it was to catch sexually transmitted infections and the importance of regular check-ups at a clinic. He also told me which mouthwash to use, the signs and symptoms of various STIs and just how serious some infections could be.

As for the security expert, he made me realise just how precarious a position I placed myself in every time I visited a client. Simple things that I'd never thought of were potentially so hazardous. It had never occurred to me that a client could easily strangle me with my own necklace. He pointed out that my shoes were completely unsuitable – how on earth could I run in slip-on high heels? It was crucial to wear shoes with an ankle strap, and shoes should never be removed unless you were with a client you had met previously and felt comfortable with. His advice had made me really think about every situation I walked into, and made me acutely aware of my surroundings. He advised that I watch how a client shut the door after me to see if he locked it and if so, how. I ensured that I never brought anything giving any personal details into a client's house or hotel room, and nothing that I couldn't afford to lose. The agency I had worked for hadn't told me any of these things. The feeling of fear as I walked to the front door of every new client was just as intense the first time as it was at my very last new booking, and so I would never knowingly let down the women who came to work for me.

My office was soon all set up and before my thoughts started to turn to frantic preparations for Christmas, I took the next step, and decided to choose a name for the agency. Of course, Christina put in her tuppenny-worth. 'If we want it to be upmarket, we need an upmarket name, like "Tiffany's" or "Truffles" or something.' I couldn't get the classic image of Audrey Hepburn in *Breakfast at Tiffany's* out of my head. She had never seemed really sexy to me. Iconic yes, but far removed from the reality of sex or even companionship. And as for Truffles, well, pigs' snouts sniffing for expensive fungus was all I could conjure up. We looked at the other agency names in the paper. Plenty beginning with 'A', just like taxi companies, mainly designed to get you at the top in listings. After all, even the Yellow Pages lists 'Escort Agencies'. Apart from this they were mostly girl's names like Sylvia's or Lolita's – presumably the type of girl you'd like to meet. Funny really, because if you took it literally, this would be the name of the madam, I suppose, rather than any escort you'd be spending time with. And, in any event, no girl would use her own name. Like 'Elite Escorts' or 'Chelsea Girls' it needed some upmarket suggestion. I thought 'Crystal' seemed to fit the bill – a bit naff, certainly, but memorable enough. I took the next step, from which there really was no turning back, and booked some advertising space in the local newspapers which would run in the New Year. And so 'Crystal Escorts' was about to be born.

Chapter Three

With the recent move and all my planning for the new agency, Christmas came around very quickly, and the whole family was looking forward to the first Christmas in our new home. The previous December, we'd managed as best we could in our cramped little rented place but this time I was determined to do better and make it special for the kids.

By 22 December, everything was pretty well organised and the presents had all been bought, wrapped and hidden away. This was always a difficult time of the year for me – had been since I was a kid. I'd watched my school friends become increasingly excited as the big day approached and wondered what it must be like to be so secure and so trusting of family life. My only experience of school holidays was the abject misery of trying to keep out of the way of my obsessively tidy mother, whilst avoiding the looming presence of my father, whose interest in me was very unwelcome.

It was my last working day before Christmas· and thankfully everything had been accomplished by then, I just had the turkey to collect. It had been a huge struggle and I had forgotten how much juggling working mums had to contend with. I was trying to fit in all the Christmas shopping with working full-time, housework, kids' activities and clubs, and trying to finish off decorating the lounge before Christmas. That evening, as I arrived home from work, I remember looking at the Christmas tree, beautifully deco-rated by the kids, absolutely full of every gaudy bauble we had, glittering with red, green and gold tinsel and every other colour under the sun. Nothing matched; we didn't go in for those sym-metrical designer Christmas trees but opted instead for the 'hang it where you can find a gap' approach. The tree sat in the bay window, which had newly glossed frames and sparkling clean windows. The windows were enormous, and I really couldn't afford curtains for them, so had instead brought several yards of voile in red and gold and dressed the window, creating an illusion which looked stunning but which had in fact been incredibly cheap. The room looked beautiful, and I was so happy that I was on holiday for nearly two weeks and had time off to enjoy everything I'd been working for.

Christmas Day itself came and went with all the usual awk-wardness of a family affected by divorce – it really is the kids who suffer. David had two children, a boy and a girl aged six and nine, and had gone to his ex's house on Christmas Eve, quite late in the evening, to share the delight that the children would undoubtedly have the following morning after seeing that Father Christmas had been. Paul turned up at about six in the morning to do the same for our children. We had decided to be grown-up and civilised, be together as a family for the sake of the kids, but in reality a very uncomfortable undercurrent prevailed. Paul left at about 8.00 pm that evening and David arrived at about 8.15 pm. David walked in the house, looking around to make sure Paul had gone. He looked so worn out and tired from the heavy emotions of the day, and I was sure that my face mirrored his. Paul was absolutely gutted over what he had lost; David was full of guilt and desperately unhappy about not being able to stay with his kids. And I found myself trying to stomach a double-helping of guilt – for taking David from his children and for not having stayed with Paul for the sake of my children's happiness. No winners at all. The following day was easier and, with the mixed emotions of Christmas Day thankfully over and David having a few days off, we relaxed and enjoyed our time together.

The weather was glorious on Boxing Day and David's two children had come to stay for the night, so off we went to the park by the river, a favourite of theirs. The kids walked to the end of the jetty and threw out copious quantities of bread; they played football, attacked one another with imaginary guns and raced around the park, timing each other to see who was the fastest. Victoria, at six years old, was valiantly trying to get to the top of the bridge of a climbing frame before any of the other kids. Suddenly she just collapsed into a sitting position. As David and I walked over to her she looked ghostly white and hardly responded when I called her name and asked her what was wrong. David lifted her from the bridge, holding her close. He put my hand on her chest and it felt like her heart was thumping its way out of her body.

Trying very, very hard not to panic and convey any of my anxiety to Victoria, we sat on a bench and she soon returned to her normal self. Her heart rate calmed down pretty quickly and all she said was that she felt butterflies inside her. I know she had been running around like mad but then she always did. She was absolutely sports mad, never still, always running, climbing – totally fearless. Victoria wanted to join in with the other children again and seemed perfectly happy, not stressed in any way, so, keeping an eye on her, we let her go back and play. It's every parent's worst nightmare when their child is ill, and the imagination does its worst and accentuates the pain with all the horrors which flash before your mind's eye. I watched Victoria's every move, every expression, just in case.

I couldn't believe this was happening, what with Victoria's other health problems – I was so scared for my poor baby. Paul and I had found out a few years before that Victoria had hearing problems. By now she was having her ears cleaned out regularly in a small operation as a day case at the local hospital. She'd had grommets inserted, but her eardrums still ruptured on occasion, and her hearing had been quite dramatically reduced from all the complications. I couldn't bear for her to have to go through anything else.

The following afternoon was rainy and rather miserable but the children were all quite happy watching a new DVD very kindly provided by Father Christmas. I went into the lounge and asked them if anyone wanted a drink, and Victoria looked at me and said, 'Mummy, the butterflies have come back.' I instantly went over and put my hand on her chest, trying to count the beats per minute. Yesterday I could understand because she had been running around like crazy, but today, sitting quietly watching TV, why the hell was her heart beating so fast? The banging in my baby's chest soon calmed and went back to normal.

I went back into the kitchen and cried as David held me – it was probably one of the worst moments of my life. Once I had calmed down and David helped me get things back into perspective, I phoned the GP and made an appointment for the next day. Dr Hillman was perfect. He must have seen this a thousand times – an overwrought mother thinking the worst – but he was wonderful and didn't make me feel anything other than so very glad that he was there. I'd known since Victoria was a baby that she had a heart murmur – it was just one of those things, and as long as school and anyone who looked after her was aware of it, everything was okay. The doctor said that we were right to worry but we should try to keep calm. He said he would refer us to a consultant paediatrician who was a cardiac specialist. Eternally grateful, we went home and Victoria, oblivious to everything, went out to play football in the mud with her brothers.

Victoria's appointment letter arrived the following week and I was horrified to see that it was for six months' time. I called the hospital and asked the consultant's secretary if there was any way Victoria could possibly see him any sooner. 'Yes, of course,' she said 'He does one day a week at the Alexandra Hospital and sees many patients privately.' I called the Alexandra and asked how soon I could see this consultant – lo and behold, there was an appointment available in three days' time. For £100 I could bypass the queue of equally anxious parents. This all felt so morally wrong, but I was not going to argue with my conscience when my daughter's health was at stake.

I called Paul; I knew he needed to be there for his baby girl. Three days later Victoria, Paul and I sat in the beautiful waiting room at the Spire Alexandra Hospital in Walderslade. There were fresh flowers on the reception desk, prints filled the walls, a state-of-the-art coffee machine invited anyone waiting to 'be my guest' without the need for a pound coin in the slot. The receptionist showed us into the office of the same paediatrician Victoria was due to see in six months' time, which still strikes me as somewhat crazy.

The doctor was delightful and had all the time in the world for us. Victoria adored him and he made everything seem so straightforward. He thought there was the possibility of something irregular going on and that Victoria might benefit from the opinion of the experts at the Royal Brompton Hospital. He said he would write to our GP and an appointment would be made. Amazingly, an appointment came through for the beginning of March – and this time it was all paid for by the NHS. So that's the trick, I guess: by paying £100 we had managed to jump a six-month waiting list. Any amount of money would have been worth it to me. I had reassurances from the consultant paediatrician that Victoria would be fine. He advised us that in the meantime, should she experience the butterflies again, give her an ice cube to suck. Apparently the intense cold instantly slows the number of heart beats down, causing the breathing and heart rate to generally return to normal. So despite constantly thinking the worst, I felt a little reassured and tried to allow Victoria to carry on as normally as I possibly could.

Victoria's health was now a priority and I knew that I could not risk being away from home every day when there was a very real chance that she could be rushed to the hospital at any time. I simply had to make Crystal Escorts work.

Just like starting any new business, there was a lot more to it than I'd first imagined. One very positive start was that my office was at home, and it looked good. I had a desk, a computer and printer, had bought lots of files and apart from that had lots of space, although for what exactly I was not quite sure. The one thing that I really needed before anything could happen at all was a very special CD. Things have moved on now, but at the time the only way to check someone really was who they said they were was to use directory enquiries or, if you could, to get hold of a CD which contained every listed phone number and address in the UK, even ex-directory ones. I had managed to acquire one of these, which was a godsend. After searching the internet and wading through various sites, I came across a company based in Holland that was offering them for sale at an exorbitant price, but that was nothing compared to the safety they brought. After my own experiences I worried so much about the girls being safe, and I was determined to do my utmost to protect them. Working as escorts was bad enough, let alone the dangers they potentially faced.

Just before Christmas I had found a very helpful lady in the form of Daphne who worked in the advertising department of the *Kent Free Ads*. She explained to me how Kent was split into seven areas as far as advertising was concerned, and very helpfully gave me the distribution figures for each area. It was £35 per ad per week, plus VAT, which made it quite an expensive business to advertise across the county. I decided to advertise in the *Maidstone Free Ads* for the first week for several reasons. The distribution was about 55,000 and Maidstone was reasonably affluent. Also, only one other escort agency advertised in that area. There was another free newspaper that went to every home in Kent but my sort of ad was considered too risqué for their readership. I drafted the wording after having looked to see what the competition had done in several newspapers, both locally and in London. After going into a newsagents, shuffling to the back of the paper like a dirty old man, then turning beetroot as the man next to me clocked the page I was looking at, I swiftly bought several papers and pondered them at home in private. From my own experience, I felt quite sure that in at least two households in my village, the men would be furtively thumbing those very same pages. Supply and demand, I thought to myself . . .

The ad would run in a small, inch-square box the first week of the New Year, and it simply read:

> Crystal Escorts
> Only to you, 7 pm – 3 am
> Escorts Always Required.
> Telephone: ***** ******

The ad made it clear that the girls would only visit them at their house or a hotel and that they only worked in the evenings (when demand was highest), since most girls were likely to have kids. And, most importantly, that we were looking for new girls. Interestingly, something that I had no idea was important at the time, is that Crystal Escorts was the only agency which advertised using a landline phone number. After plenty of rewriting, I was quietly impressed that I managed to do this in so few words.

In spite of my planning, all the what-ifs kept coming back to me. What if no clients rang? What if no girls rang for jobs? What if I saw myself sitting there all night without the phone ringing? In fact, that's exactly what happened on our first night of business. The ad appeared in the edition of the paper which came out between Christmas and New Year, but I hadn't been expecting to see it until the first week of January. Christina received her copy before I got mine and came hurrying over with it. At first I didn't notice the awful mistake, which thankfully was not my fault or Daphne's, but a slip-up by one of the copywriters. The phone number had been printed with two digits the wrong way around, so a family in Strood were being inundated by weird phone calls – calls from men who wanted to make their own Christmas a little happier, but were in fact ruining someone else's! I rang the number as it appeared in the ad, and a woman answered the phone. I explained that I owned Crystal Escorts and began to launch into an awkward apology. Luckily the woman saw the funny side and said they'd had quite a giggle about it – thank goodness for Christmas spirit, I thought. In fact, they had been in touch with the newspaper, who confirmed that somewhere along the chain the number had been written incorrectly. The family did rather well out of it – the woman told me they had been given pantomime tickets and a night out by way of an apology. As far as lost business was concerned, I figured it was one of those things not worth getting your knickers in a twist over. I just wanted it put right as soon as possible. So, after a word with Daphne, who gave us two weeks' free advertising, we were on track again. The ad reappeared with the correct number and the phone would soon be heard.

I was taking such a massive step in starting this agency, taking such a chance on its success and all that it would mean. Christina had made her decision to become an escort and I was facilitating that decision. I felt such a mixture of right and wrong. Was I actually encouraging her to do this, to face all the experiences that I had managed to get away from, and perpetrating even more misery? Christina had decided for her own reasons and entirely on her own that she needed to earn money quickly, and told me she was going to become an escort whether I was involved or not – after all, there were plenty of other agencies around. If it wasn't me then it would be someone else, and I was determined that Crystal Escorts would be different from the rest. For one thing, my girls would be safe, of that I was certain.

Crunch time had arrived – the first day of a new year and the first day of business for Crystal Escorts. At 7.00 pm I sat in the office, with Christina all done up to the nines, and we waited.

The first time the phone rang I looked at it until Christina said, 'Well, pick the bloody thing up then!'

'Crystal Escorts, can I help you?'

As it was just me and Christina, and I was only the telephonist, the whole thing felt like a bit of a joke at this point, more like a *Carry On* film than anything else. I guess it's like any other start-up business: you can't be afraid to bluff a little.

I had come up with a range of identities for Christina, within reason, of course. So, when David from Maidstone rang – could I send someone over to him and who was working tonight? – I thought it would cover all possibilities to turn the question around. So my stock response became, 'What sort of lady are you looking for?' He asked for 'a blonde', which Christina certainly was, 'in her mid-20s', which she most certainly wasn't. Rather stunned by this first call, I took David's landline number and his address, and told him I would make the arrangements, then call him back to confirm. The last thing I asked him was the name of the person the telephone was registered to. A client might very well say his name was Joe Bloggs and that he lived wherever, but I had to be as sure as I possibly could before I sent anyone to that address. That way, the client knew we had something connecting them to their address – a chain to follow should anything untoward happen. After the check, I phoned David back and told him that Christina would be with him in about 30 minutes.

'Right then, I suppose I'd better be on my way.' Her supreme confidence meant the age thing didn't worry her but Christina suddenly looked anxious, and I knew exactly what was going through her mind.

'Look, love, you don't have to do this if you don't want to,' I said, and I meant it. 'It doesn't matter. I can always call him back and make up an excuse. There's plenty more agencies out there, he's hardly going to mind.' I couldn't bear it if she felt I was coercing her in some way.

'No, no, I'm going, it'll be fine.' Christina picked up her bag, reached for her coat and was on her way to the front door. Nothing but determination showed on her face.

'Christina, wait. Listen, remember, you must phone me when you get there to let me know he's okay and I'll call you exactly an hour later to let you know you have to leave. Don't switch off your phone. And, if there's anything, *anything* at all that doesn't feel right, just leave. You don't have to say a word, just get out. Remember, he's likely to be far more nervous than you. Oh, and don't tell him your real name.'

As I watched her drive off, I imagined every step of Christina's journey to Maidstone. I felt sick for her, remembering so clearly the emotions that had rampaged through me as I knocked on my first client's door. Christina had momentarily looked petrified; just for one second that look of terror had shown on her face, but she'd shoved it away and compartmentalised the fear. Her family was her priority, and remembering that was when determination replaced her fear. I wanted to scream at her to come back, that it was all a mistake, that the whole idea was crazy, but it was too late because she had found her way to make it through, just as I had several years before.

The phone rang again almost as soon as Christina had driven off, and I found myself having to pretend that we were terribly busy that night. I reassured callers that we would be more than happy to hear from them again. There wasn't much more I could do, feeble though it must have sounded. One chap phoned and asked me to describe a girl who might be available. As the call went on, I thought I could hear a breathless edge to his speech. Unnaturally long pauses followed the answers I gave to his increasingly detailed questions. Rather stupidly, it took me a while to cotton on to what he was up to. I suddenly had a picture of a lonely middle-aged man, in front of the TV, volume down. He's thumbed through the local freebie paper – at first looking at a second-hand lawnmower or PC for sale. Then his eyes, mind, and eventually his hand, all wander as he sees 'Personal Services', Any pity I felt evaporated as I remembered what business I was in – it was an escort agency, not a chat line, and all he was doing was stopping my clients getting through. There were plenty of premium-rate chat lines out there, if he was that desperate. Click. I just put the phone down. And that course of action became my policy. Sometimes it happened again and again, the same guy, and every time I just put the handset down, hoping he'd eventually get bored and get his kicks some other way.

Christina phoned me 30 minutes later to tell me that she was just about to knock on David's door and my heart leapt into my mouth as I remembered my very first experience, that first-ever job, having sex with my first stranger for money. That memory – the whole experience – will remain with me forever. Just before the hour was up and I'd had a chance to call, Christina rang again and said she was on her way back, and that everything had been fine.

When she came in, I could see how relieved she was. Here was the old Christina back again, describing the experience almost without a care in the world, as if it were something she had been doing for years. Her toughness amazed me. I didn't exactly go to pieces after my first time but neither did I feel exactly happy or unburdened about what I'd done, merely relieved, as the money I had made would make such a huge difference. David, the man she had seen, was a telephone engineer who had, he told her, split up with his girlfriend and just wanted some company. As predicted, he'd been terribly nervous and, in spite of the fact that Christina wasn't quite the 20-something girl of his dreams, the mere fact that she was apparently highly attracted to him and willing to jump straight into bed with him had more than compensated for the age difference! And, yes, as ever, the one-hour booking was over in around 40 minutes. She smiled at me with a look of utter joy.

'You do realise, don't you, that the £120 I've just made means I can actually go to the supermarket tomorrow and pay for my shopping in cash instead of sticking it on yet another credit card?' Yes, I knew exactly how she felt. Like she was already beginning to claw back control of her life.

Christina was only back in the office for 20 minutes or so before the phone rang again and she was off, to a place just up the road with a chap who, we both felt sure, was rather practised in the art of calling escort agencies. His phone number had checked out and once again Christina had promised me faithfully that she'd call in to let me know she was okay.

I looked at the phone hoping it wouldn't ring again since I'd already made a firm decision that two bookings was quite enough for Christina on her first night. So many agencies just work you and work you until you can barely keep your eyes open. If you refuse to take bookings, they threaten you with no work ever again, or they start giving your best customers to other girls so that you end up seeing a string of horrible creeps who have devoted their lives to calling up escorts and treating them like shit.

It was now around 10.30 pm and Christina had called to say that all had been well and to ask where she should go next. 'Home,' I said, laughing. 'Let's call it a night.' I was just about to switch the phone to the answer machine when it rang again. But this time, the voice was that of a woman.

'Is that Crystal Escorts?' she whispered.

'Yes,' I said trying to sound professional. 'Can I help you?'

'It's about your advert. I was wondering. Are you still looking for escorts?'

'Yes, yes, we are.' I stuttered. 'Um . . . tell me a bit about yourself.' I knew I sounded ridiculous, after all, I was hardly interviewing her for a conventional job. Her response wasn't quite what I'd expected.

'I can't really stay on the phone now. Could we meet up for a coffee or something, tomorrow maybe?'

I took Jenny's details and arranged to meet her two days later at a local wine bar. Trying to sound very relaxed and informal, I had joked and invited her along for a coffee or a brandy, depending on how nervous she was. Holly didn't feel the need to meet me before I started working for her agency, even though I asked. I was determined to do things very differently.

I was in a dilemma about my day job. I had to give a month's notice but, not quite believing that this could all work, I had hesitated every time I'd gone to give my letter to the personnel department before Christmas. I kept going over what I would do if the agency didn't work out as I had no hope of paying the mortgage with no job. I knew I could go back to Simon at the employment agency and get another secretarial job in London, but the money just wouldn't be enough. My worst-case scenario chilled me in an instant – that I might feel my only option was to go back to prostitution myself. I had originally planned to work during the days and somehow struggle through the nights until I was sure the agency was going well enough to hand in my notice. Now with Victoria's health problems, I felt a strong need to be at home during the day so I could be nearby if anything happened to her. I played through all the options in my mind, and decided to take one step at a time. I know it was wrong, but I decided I'd just phone in sick. After four hours sleep and the hectic readying of the kids, I'd probably sound suitably rough on the phone anyway.

The next morning I rang in and said that I had flu, and wouldn't be in – probably for a few days – but would stay in touch. That night, the phone rang constantly; Christina went out to visit two clients, which made the decision for me. At 9.00 am the following day, prickling with apprehension at the idea of jacking in a fairly well-paid, stable job, I rang the personnel officer and told her that I was sorry but couldn't cope, and wouldn't be coming back. They weren't terribly amused and I did feel bad about it. But it would have been impossible to try to continue as I had been, and would be unfair to the kids, especially Victoria, not to mention everyone else. I was so relieved to have it out of the way, but also aware that another step had just been taken into the unknown.

Later that morning, as I sat in the dark interior of our local wine bar, a very nervous-looking girl fitting the description Jenny had given walked towards me.

'Dawn?'

'Yes,' I said, smiling, and got up to shake her hand. 'Here, sit down.'

I got us both a drink, trying to calm her down as she was obviously so nervous. Christ, I've been there, love, standing up in my new high heels whilst a pimp walked around me, looking me up and down before delivering his verdict. Oh yes, Jenny, I know exactly how you must be feeling. She told me she was 28 and, when I asked why she wanted to work, she told me she had two kids, aged five and three; she'd split up with their dad a couple of years ago and things had just gone from bad to worse. Jenny lived on a notorious council estate in Gravesend, which was a haven for dealers. Several of the flats in her block were occupied by addicts and the fighting and general mayhem that had become a feature of her everyday life were beginning to drive her to despair. She was desperate to move out, to get on a housing association scheme – anything to get away from an environment that might, who knew, eventually claim her sanity or, worse, the lives of her children. When her washing machine had broken down six months ago and there'd been no money for a new one, she'd borrowed money from a local lender and, surprise, surprise, was now so behind with the repayments that she had nowhere to turn. And so she turned to me.

I hadn't prepared myself for this. She was so desperate and, in spite of the fact that she was a pretty, nicely dressed young girl, I didn't know if she had the self-confidence that she'd need to put up with all the crap she'd encounter if she started working. She sat there, with her long dark hair framing her face, spinning a thin silver ring on her middle finger, willing me to help her out.

'I just don't know, love.' I said. 'You have to understand that this isn't necessarily easy money. What about a part-time job? Can't you get some help with the children?'

But of course she'd thought about that and, with her very limited skills and her very pressing debt issue, this girl was looking for a solution now, today even. She reassured me that she knew what it was all about, that she'd thought it through, and she'd even managed to persuade her neighbour to mind the children a couple of nights a week whilst she worked. She had told them she'd got a night job at a petrol station. No one bothered to challenge her. They probably knew.

'Okay,' I said. 'Give it some thought and then phone me. If you're sure, then yes, we'll talk again.' Only three hours later my mobile phone rang, and the following night Jenny started work.

I sensed Jenny's naïvety despite the fact that she'd grown up in a very hard part of Gravesend, and there was something about her which suggested that given an opportunity, Jenny would be a very different person. She had aspirations and she wanted to break the mould and offer her children a better start in life than she'd been given. I very carefully went through all the safety tips I'd gone through with Christina, and would make a habit of doing with all the girls. The need to have your phone with you at all times. Don't wear jewellery that could be pulled or used to hurt you. Keep your shoes on and make sure you always have a change of clothes in the car, just in case you need to make a run for it. Make sure the client doesn't lock the bedroom door. And, most importantly, if you sense something is wrong, make your excuses and leave.

There were also 'tricks of the trade' to make life easier when having your period. Even though the man is a client, not a lover, it certainly adds nothing to the experience except embarrassment, and can be downright uncomfortable. At that time of the month you'd rather be stacking shelves, typing in the dullest office – anything rather than escorting. In an ideal world, you'd just take a few days off – but then there's the money. And, if you were a girl who'd constructed a cover job, how do you explain to your partner, friends or children how you can regularly take three days off? No, we just used to find ways of limiting the problem.

A no-brainer was to use the bathroom on arriving at a client's home or hotel room. Tidy up, remove the tampon, wash and douche and generally clean up as much as possible. Take a natural sponge, about ping-pong ball sized, and rinse it through with warm, clean water. Then squeeze KY jelly through it, pop it in and that usually did the trick. Also, use red condoms for this time of the month. That way, if there was any leakage it would be much less likely to show up.

Then we moved onto the health issues and I ran through the catalogue of horrid diseases and infections that could so easily be picked up. I looked at Jenny and asked her if she understood everything and still wanted to continue – definitely, she said, but added that she had no idea that half of these diseases existed, let alone how to spot if you had them or where to go for a check-up.

Finally, a few additional golden rules to protect herself emotionally. I told Jenny the complications involved in letting a client develop feelings for you and vice versa: never become emotionally involved – it really was not worth the hassle because that's what it would become, a problem. Use a false name and don't give away too many details about yourself or your private life. I told her about a client I used to have who had made it his business to discover as much about me as possible and who had actually told his wife he was leaving her and arrived on my doorstep! Jenny was horrified and agreed that she would always take what she was told with a pinch (or a small bucket) of salt. I went on to tell her never to give a client a lift anywhere, drop something off for them or collect anything. We worked through the list and Jenny seemed to understand everything she'd been told.

I had this overwhelming urge to open my purse and tell her to go to Tesco's on the way home, on me. It was clear that my perspective on the whole enterprise was changing. My first thoughts about running an escort agency had been, if I'm honest about it, largely selfish. I wanted to continue to provide a happy and stable life for my kids, and needed a good income to do it. So the agency idea seemed like the answer. Christina could, I thought, take care of herself, but Jenny really brought home to me how desperate women's lives can get. For all I knew, she was perhaps once a bright and promising kid doing well at school. But it only takes a few let-downs, perhaps a home life that doesn't support school work, money problems, and then, before you know it, that same bright kid is raising children of her own with no future at all.

This wasn't at all the way I'd planned it. I was convinced that I'd made a terrible mistake and that Jenny would turn out to be far too wounded and vulnerable to stand the pressures of the job.

Chapter Four

Crystal Escorts was doing well, and thanks to the ads I'd now met up with four other girls. Three of them fitted the bill and I began to feel like we were on the way to making the agency a success. My days were spent doing all the things that stay-at-home mothers do, and yet no matter how much I tidied, cleaned, washed and ironed, I still found myself running around trying to keep ahead of the demands of the family. I'll never understand how you can make more time for the house, but you end up with even less time for yourself.

A few weeks after my first meeting with Jenny, she'd already proved me as wrong as I could have been and was now working two nights a week, taking five or six bookings in total, and suddenly her life was transformed. With weekly earnings of around £700, even after she'd paid the agency commission, she was now beginning to turn her life around.

Although we were still a tiny agency operating in a huge sea populated with much bigger fish, I already had a fairly good list of regular clients who appreciated the fact that I was straightforward, friendly on the phone and honest. Other agencies would have a standard policy of saying the girl would be there 'in 45 minutes', even when there was no way she'd be there for at least two hours. Two hours is not what a lusty client wants to hear, but at least he knows where he stands. If you tell him 45 minutes, you'll have one frustrated client. And to my thinking it was extremely unfair to put a girl in front of a client who already thinks it must be her fault she's an hour and a quarter late.

From the point of view of the girls, our way of working meant the risk factor was minimised, and so far every bloke they'd been to see, short or tall, fat or thin, was at least as normal as you might expect. These guys might not always be sophisticated, and quite a few of them were about as useless at love-making as they clearly were at housework, but their sexual prowess (or lack of it) was not the reason we were there. So Jenny, having spent several hours in the company of an assorted bunch of plumbers, accountants, sales executives and one dental hygienist, had managed to pay off her loan and had gas and electricity to last her the month. She'd even managed to paint her front room and buy new duvet covers for her boys. She was almost unrecognisable; her once lanky hair was now shiny and you could hardly wipe the smile off her face. I was pleased for her, but I knew that she had big plans, and saving enough to move out of the flat was her priority now.

One Tuesday morning I headed off to the supermarket to do what was meant to be a month's stocking up on essentials. Mondays to Wednesdays were usually very quiet for the agency – single men tended to wait until the end of the week for their 'entertainment'; and those with wives and girlfriends at home found it difficult to make time for themselves at the start of the week. I rummaged in my purse for a pound coin for the trolley – why did I never ever have one? And why did some smug woman standing behind me always have one of those trolley tokens attached to her organised key ring? Christina would have had a token, I grinned to myself, as I queued for change from the cigarette kiosk. She would also, it occurred to me, be adding new items to her trolley – condoms, wipes, cheap stockings, KY Jelly, baby oil . . . The lady whose trolley token I so coveted had already waltzed off and was probably consulting her neatly written list, ordered according to the precise layout of the store.

Me? I started at the beginning then wandered up and down every aisle, endlessly retracing my steps as I remembered other bits and pieces I needed to buy. I headed back to the fresh-food section for some carrots and there, amongst the fruit and veg, picking out new potatoes, was my mother. I hadn't seen this woman for seven years – she had never even met my three youngest children. My mother, here in Rochester, buying potatoes. I stood, frozen to the spot, unable to take my eyes away from this woman who right now created in me the biggest bag of mixed emotions. Maybe she sensed something because she suddenly looked straight at me. She didn't look any different; she still had sleek long red hair, which she wore swept up at the side with combs. The thoughts that went through my head seemed to take hours to feed through – the feelings of rejection, bitterness, anger, love – but of course it was only seconds. All we could do was say hello to each other, no hug, no touching – there never had been. There was no scene, no recriminations, nothing. My mother. She asked me how the children were. I told her that Deborah was a redhead just like her and made some sort of pathetic joke about it being a constant reminder. I craved her love, this hard woman, my mother who had never acknowledged what had happened to me in my childhood. Just for her to say she believed me when I told her that my father had abused me, would have made it all okay. I wanted so much to have a mother who loved me, like my best friend and her mum. All this mind-blowing emotion, experienced with a bunch of carrots in my hand. I had been hurt by her so many times before; let down because she could not say what I needed to hear. Why I didn't walk away the second I spotted her I don't know.

The children were taking part in a school sports competition at 2.00 pm that afternoon and, almost without thinking, I asked my mother if she would like to come and see them. I explained it was nothing special, not like the annual summer sports day, just a bit of fun really – relay races, long jump, that sort of thing. As I was about to tell her the name and address of the school, she interrupted me.

'It's all right, Dawn, I know where the school is. I'll be there.'

And that was it. Nothing. No questions about me, no mention of how well I looked, or asking how Paul was doing. She'd been out of my life for seven years by now and yet she knew where the children, three of whom she'd never met, went to school. Did it mean she secretly cared, that she'd kept a watchful eye on us from afar? I clung to the idea that she did love us after all. She walked away and I carried on round the store, chucking random stuff into the trolley, things I'd never normally buy. Memories of my childhood came flooding back – the cruelty, the absence of affection, the years of yearning for her love and acceptance.

The tears came in torrents and I had to get out. I called David and told him through sobs what had happened. Nothing. And that was the problem. He is very practical, sensible and calmed me down, saying he would meet me at the school that afternoon, just to be there and hold my hand. David could have no way of understanding how much this all meant to me. I was never very good at explaining things like this to him, and he would get in-furiated with me when I was upset and he didn't know why. It was like I couldn't find the words to explain and I didn't even want to put the feelings into words, because there was absolutely nothing anyone could do anyway.

I walked over to the café area and left my trolley to one side, bought a horrible cup of coffee and phoned my friend, Gillian. It wasn't really to talk but merely to connect with someone who knew what I was feeling because we had grown up together, been friends since we were ten years old. Gillian would understand how I was feeling just by my telling her that I had seen my mother. It wasn't that I wanted sympathy or attention, it was that the shock of seeing her had zapped every ounce of my strength. All the memories of this person who had hurt me so badly over the years had been scooped up and put in a box on a high shelf somewhere in the recesses of my mind, never to be opened. But now, this afternoon, I felt that ache again, and I wanted someone to understand, someone who knew how much I had just wanted my mum. Gillian was at work, but she stopped what she was doing, closed her office door and listened to me quietly crying in Tesco, as I told her between sobs that my heart was breaking all over again. I drank the dreadful coffee and wiped my face, thanked Gillian with all my heart for being my friend, and finally promised her that I was okay and back in sensible mum-to-my-kids mode.

Putting the mobile back on the table, I took in my surroundings again. Life, grocery shopping, the people behind me, it was all going on without a ruffle. Even if someone had seen me in my emotional mess, they would likely have politely ignored me. That's how we've trained ourselves. Thank goodness for mobile phones; they keep us connected with a select few and insulated from those who are right next to us.

I collected the trolley and raced around the shop, aware that I needed to hurry and get the groceries home and unpacked in double-quick time or I would be late for the sports event. After parting with what seemed like half the national debt and carting two overflowing trolley loads of dog food, soap powder and all the other things that make up our daily lives into the car, I drove home feeling weak and angry. I only had a couple of hours before I had to leave for school and so I tried as hard as I could to close the box of painful memories, for the rest of the day at least.

Scooby brought me out of my state of deep thought with his persistent barking. 'Good boy,' I told him as I walked to the front door. Maybe a walk would sort me out. As I hunted for his lead in the kitchen drawer, Christina, in her own special way, bustled in, filling up the house with her presence. 'Coffee, darling?' I recall her saying as she marched over to the sink to fill the kettle. With one eye on the time, I asked her if all was okay. I wanted to give her the opportunity to get off her chest whatever it was she had obviously come to tell me. Then she dropped her bombshell and I listened, thinking, oh great, now what do I do? Christina had decided, as a seasoned professional with a whole six weeks' experience of being an escort, that she would put her own ad in the paper, alongside the Crystal Escorts ad. She would only do outcalls and hopefully still be able to work for me too. Her plan was to be available for me but if she had a call to her number she would take that first, as obviously she wouldn't have a booking fee to pay.

'Why? What's happened? Are you okay? Did something happen at the weekend?' I was stunned. What had brought about this sudden turn of events? Had I let her down? Was she angry with me?

'Nothing's happened, Dawn, it's just that frankly, with you only looking after the phones in the evening, I'm standing around all day twiddling my thumbs when, if you think about it, I could actually be working.'

She had a point and I suppose if she preferred to work during the daytime that was her prerogative.

Call Me Madam

'Look, Christina, I can't stop you but please think about what you're doing. At least we know a lot of the blokes that call the agency, and we can check their phone numbers and make sure you're not going somewhere unsafe. These ads, well, how will you know if the client's okay or not? Anything could happen.'

'Anything could happen with your callers, Dawn. Let's face it – it's not foolproof. I have got to make some serious money in the next couple of months. Gerry isn't going to get another job and we're in deep trouble. I'm sorry, it's nothing personal, but if I don't get out there we are going to lose the house.'

How could I argue with her? I was fielding as many bookings as I could but the agency just didn't have the profile yet to generate the kind of earnings that Christina needed – she wasn't like Jenny, it wasn't hundreds of pounds a week she needed to dig her out of debt, but thousands.

Christina's ad came out next week on the Wednesday so we would carry on as normal until then and she would let me know what sort of response she was getting. Knowing that she probably wouldn't listen to me anyway, I printed off the names and addresses of half a dozen or so of the serious weirdos that I knew of. These ranged from a couple of addresses that hadn't checked out or didn't exist on the electoral roll search, to one man who I had been sent to by Holly a couple of years ago who had attacked me. Christina was true to form and just glanced at the sheet of paper and folded it away in her bag. She picked up our cups and put them in the dishwasher, then breezed off as if she had just arranged a hairdressing appointment.

I gave up any thoughts of a walk and let Scooby out into the garden instead. I put a tracksuit on and found my trainers, bag and coat, grabbed some after-school snacks and drinks, and eventually the car keys – on the hook where they should be but the last place I looked. Trying to cope with the emotions of the re-emergence of my mother coupled with Christina's announcement was giving me a headache, so I swallowed a couple of paracetamol and drove to school. David rang to say he would be about 20 minutes and, if I wanted to, I could just to wait in the car for him and we would meet her together. I laughed, telling him he could occasionally be quite nice!

I parked up and saw Debbie, my scatty, lovely friend, waving to me so I wandered over to join her. Debbie was mum to four boys and married to a lovely man called Jeff. Debbie's son, Chip, and my Victoria were best friends at school and spent much of their free time together too. Debbie made me laugh, was so care-free, and had a knack of finding something positive in the most dire of situations. She was a dependable and loyal friend whom I loved dearly. As we chatted, David came up behind me and kissed me. I was so relieved to be with him; it gave me strength to deal with the emotions of the afternoon ahead.

And then I saw her. She was alone but seemed quite confident as she parked and put her coat on, fished about in her car for an umbrella and looked around – for me I guess. I nodded at the woman walking towards me and, as much to steel myself as to identify her, said to Debbie and David, 'My mother.' After the introductions, Debbie tactfully slipped off and watched her kids with some other friends. David stood to one side of my mother and looked at me questioningly, mouthing out 'Do you want me to go?' but I clung to his hand – I didn't want to be on my own with her. I couldn't read her at all as she watched five of her grandchildren playing sport, three of whom she had never even seen before. What had I expected?

As the children ran races, crawled through hoops and did various other activities, I pointed out each of them to my mother. She clapped at the appropriate times and watched with interest as Victoria won every race she entered, commenting on how like my sister, Joanne, she was. As the games finished, the children found their respective parents and mine all looked inquisitively at this woman with me. I introduced my children to their grandmother. Deborah, aged eight, was quite fascinated to meet the woman whom she felt was responsible for saddling her with red hair and a lifetime of negative ginger comments. Tea was being served in the conservatory of the school and, whilst the children went to the changing rooms to slip back into their school uniforms, David, my mother and I queued with the other parents for a cup of tea. The children found us again, and, whilst drinking their juice, politely answered their grandmother's questions.

After about ten minutes my mother announced that she had to go and find her husband, who was visiting a friend, as they were flying back to Germany, where they lived, the following morning. She would be back in England soon and would perhaps catch up with us again if that was okay, and she would call me to organise it. She said goodbye quite formally to all the children, told David how nice it had been to meet him, and that was it. She said goodbye to me, turned and walked away. This totally unexpected reunion was abruptly over, as quickly as it had come about.

David squeezed my hand as I watched her drive off. 'Not now, love,' he said. 'We'll talk about it later. Don't cry. Is she really worth all these tears?'

What is it they say about not being able to choose your family? All I had ever wanted for my kids was this perfect Enid Blyton-style existence, complete with doting Granny and lovely old Grandpa with his pipe and slippers making it all perfect, but the reality was far from it. Paul's mother was only interested in her son and the children were just a by-product of an unsuitable relationship. She had never been the granny type, more the 'turn up and kiss the children, but please don't put your jammy, felt-tip fingers all over my Armani, darling' variety. And my mother was the ice queen in denial. Or maybe it was just me, seeking something that simply had never existed.

We went home to the usual pandemonium. School bags dumped in the middle of the hallway, me screaming at them to move their things, Scooby barking for a walk and then about three minutes quiet as the kids ate their supper. Homework completed, reading done and spellings tested, netball knickers found and rugby boots retrieved from muddy kitbag, the three youngest finally went to bed and Alexander was off watching TV. Peace and quiet finally fell over the house as I pottered around the kitchen emptying draws and cupboards in an attempt to tidy and sort their contents – anything to take my mind away from the emotional events of the day. About an hour had passed and I had managed some semblance of order when I looked up and saw Emily and Alice standing in the doorway. It was Alice who spoke first. I think I knew what she was going to say but I didn't interrupt or try to pre-empt, I just let her speak.

'Mum?'

'Yes, Alice.'

'Why didn't you say that Grandma was coming to watch us at school today?' Nothing more, nothing odd, just a simple question. But it opened the floodgates all over again.

There were lots of questions. They wanted to know why she was here and what she wanted. I asked the girls to give me half an hour and then I would sit down with them and explain. Tonight was Tuesday, David's night for going to see his children. Ever since he had split with Laura, he had visited his kids every Tuesday and Thursday for a couple of hours in the evening. He tried so hard to maintain this regular contact with the kids and tonight he asked me if I wanted him to stay with me whilst I spoke to the girls. I knew how much it meant to him to see his own children and he didn't give up his Tuesdays and Thursdays lightly. I told him we would be fine, that he was to go and see his own children and I would see him later. Emily, Alice and I sat down together and I prepared myself for the barrage of questions that would surely come. I explained how I had bumped into my mother whilst shopping and had on the spur of the moment invited her to the school. Emily said that she could vaguely remember her from years ago.

Both girls knew that I had had a terrible relationship with my parents, and I have always tried to be as open and honest with them as I could about my childhood. Talking about abuse and having to admit to the fact that my first sexual experience had been most unwelcome is so difficult. How do you tell your children that this sort of thing goes on and simultaneously reassure them that you're normal? It's hardly the stuff of fireside reminiscences. I remembered my father's funeral and standing at the graveside, crying with a mixture of love and hate for him at the same time.

The girls also knew that my mother had reacted strongly when I finally told her about my father's abuse, so strongly in fact that I was terrified. Instead of comforting me and talking to me, she simply filed for divorce and more or less ignored me from that day onwards. The only time she even acknowledged the abuse I had suffered at the hands of my father was when she wanted to gain custody of my younger brother and sister – she used it as a bargaining tool, so she could scare him into giving her what she wanted. And even then, she maintained that she still didn't believe me.

The problem with secrets and lies is that they always have a way of coming out, of emerging when you least expect it and I didn't want any of the children to learn about their granddad from a third party. I wanted to tell them myself in a matter-of-fact way that could not be misconstrued or misunderstood. I vividly remember Alexander drawing a family tree for his homework and asking me about my father. His questions were innocent childish enquiries but, as we sat having dinner that day, the memories I had tried so hard to block overwhelmed me. Alexander asked me what year my father had died, as he needed to fill in the gaps in his tree. Then he asked how he'd died and in that moment, like any parent faced with this situation, I had to make a very quick decision – do I tell the truth about something that was really quite awful or do I try to gloss over it and make everything sound normal?

I decided to tell the truth, worrying that it would do more damage in the long run not to. I came straight out with it and told them that he had killed himself in his car, parked at the side of the motorway. He had run a pipe from the exhaust into the car and had died of carbon monoxide poisoning. The children said little, but then came the 'Why?', as I knew it would. At that point I decided that Alexander was too young to know and chose not to tell him, saying I wasn't really sure and then changing the subject. But later that evening I told the two older girls, explaining that I didn't want to say anything so terrible in front of Alexander because I wasn't sure he would understand anyway. The girls were clearly upset and very sad for me, as I was for them, for having to make sense of something as awful as this.

They coped very well, and I told them that it obviously wasn't something I particularly wanted to talk about but if they ever had any questions about our family then they must ask me.

Seeing their grandmother again must have been a bit weird for them, but I said that they weren't to worry, that I had more than enough on my mind without my mother coming back to complicate matters. We were okay as we were. And so, off they went, reassured, back to their worlds of music and boys, homework and friends. And I was even more determined that nothing so awful would ever taint their lives. But the time would come when I would have to have the one conversation with each of the children that I truly dreaded. After all, telling your children that not only were you sexually abused, but that you then went on to work as an escort, was not a conversation for which there were any precedents. No amount of explaining how much in debt we'd been, or any of the other details, was going to save me from having to look each and every one of them in the eye and tell them *that* particular truth.

Chapter Five

*T*hursday evening, 8.30 pm. The phone rings.

'Hello, is that Crystal Escorts?'

'Yes, sir,' I reply promptly. 'Can I help you?'

'I hope so. I was wondering if you might have a young lady who would like to spend a couple of hours with me at home, nothing special, just a bit of company was all I was after.'

I couldn't place the voice at first, but when he gave his name as Tom and an address I suddenly remembered. Ah, *that* Tom. This was a chap who booked me almost every night when I was working. He was a big guy, to put it mildly, and, to be clear, I'm talking about his waist. He was absolutely huge, and one of the nicest, most charming people I had ever met. I knew Jenny would be okay. I took the usual booking details and told Tom I would call back to confirm. I dialled Jenny's number, gave her the address, adding that I knew this man personally and although he was really quite large it would be fine, he would pay her in cash and as far as clients went he was one of the best. I thought I owed it to her to explain one more thing. His obesity meant she would probably not have to actually have sex with him.

I called Tom back and told him a delightful lady called 'Lisa' would be with him in about half an hour. At 11.30 pm Jenny rang and the tone of her voice was pure joy. Tom had been wonderful, funny, polite and just thoroughly decent. She said he had a fabulous house but they had spent the evening drinking champagne in his hot tub in the garden. All she'd had to do was massage him and he was perfectly happy. They talked about everything under the sun and Tom told her all about his years spent working abroad. She said she thought he was lonely. It's funny how that was always the one overriding emotion I always picked up from the clients I had visited. For a guy like Tom, sustaining a relationship with a woman was virtually impossible. The fact that he was so overweight had effectively taken him right out of the dating game and he no longer had any self-confidence at all. Instead of risking humiliation by asking a girl for a date, only to be laughed at, he had discovered the joys of using an escort service. Tom knew that the women who visited him wouldn't laugh or appear disgusted by his physical shape. Provided he remained as charming as he always was when I used to visit him, there would be plenty of women who would be more than happy to spend a few hours in his company. As far as I was concerned, it was a win-win situation, though of course at the end of the day, he still had to face the possibility that he might never marry or find his soulmate.

Call Me Madam

Whilst Jenny had been luxuriating in the bubbles with Tom, and the three or four other girls who worked their regular dates were waving their magic wands across the county, Christina had set off for Aylesford to see a Mr Gregson at a hotel.

Hotel bookings can occasionally be tricky because there is a greater opportunity for a client to use his imagination to fulfil a fantasy. I once turned up to a very posh hotel near the Dartford Tunnel to find a very nervous young man, Charles, who explained to me that this was his stag night and the following weekend he was getting married. After a few minutes I heard a sniggering and from behind the curtains out came a very sociable young man called Nigel, somewhat under the influence but very pleasant, embarrassed and also very excited at the prospect of a real live 'lady of the night'. The plot thickened when another public-schooled young man emerged from the wardrobe, and a couple more from the bathroom. All told, there was me and seven chaps who were all pissed as newts but very happy and jovial. Nigel seemed to take the lead and asked the boys to have a whip-round for me. So after deciding that they were completely terrified of me and that they were also completely harmless, I put some music on and did what I hoped passed for a sexy striptease on the coffee table. Those of the stag party still remotely interested and/or capable were then treated to about five minutes of intimacy in the privacy of the bathroom. It was all quite good-natured and funny. In hindsight it could have been a horrific situation. Thank goodness it wasn't.

As far as I could tell, it was all above board and Christina was due to stay with Mr Gregson for two hours. Just an hour into the booking, she called to say she was on her way home. A few minutes later Mr Gregson rang. He didn't exactly complain, just said that he felt that the lady he had spent the past hour with was more like a school teacher than an escort and next time could he see someone less intimidating, please? Oh well, at least he wanted there to be a next time. On the one hand I found it funny, but on the other I wondered what had happened. Had Christina been scared by him? Had he perhaps said something that had creeped her out? I called her back. No, she was adamant, nothing had gone wrong but that in her view Mr Gregson was such a drip that she couldn't be bothered so she'd literally galloped through the massage, before, by the sound of her description, approaching sex rather as you might set about winning first prize in the local gymkhana. All very efficient but not exactly sensual. I couldn't stop laughing; after all, there's nothing in the rule book that says you can't apply a little discipline occasionally. Sadly, Mr Gregson had not appreciated her approach to the sensual arts and, though he did phone again, he begged me to find him someone a little gentler!

Later that night, I took a call from someone who just said her name was Marie and who wanted to meet up as soon as possible. She didn't want to talk on the phone but by now I was used to this. The air of paranoia every time a girl phoned was so evident – they were terrified of being overheard and it was almost as though they couldn't admit to themselves they were making the call. I did my best to put Marie at ease and suggested in as light-hearted manner as I could that we meet the next day in The Cellar Wine Bar on Rochester High Street at around lunchtime.

I took another booking for Jenny that night, another for Christina and then, finally, at around two in the morning, with the girls on their way back to their respective homes, I unplugged the phone and flopped into bed, feeling that the evening had gone pretty well. David had not come back to my house that night as he knew I would be answering the phone until the early hours and would only wake him up when I came to bed. He was a light sleeper and had a really early start on work days so I didn't want to disturb him. Still, this job was playing havoc with our relationship.

The next day, I met Marie as planned. When I walked in I spotted a woman sitting at a table in the corner of the wine bar. She'd told me on the phone she was 46 but as I drew closer I couldn't believe it. She looked so young!

I had asked her to dress as she thought she would have to for this kind of work. How on earth she had managed to balance in those shoes I shall never know. Bearing in mind she'd had to walk through the High Street I had to give her top marks for effort. Marie had teamed her impossible heels with a pair of black fishnets, pillar-box red lipstick and the shortest mini-skirt I have ever seen in Rochester on a Saturday at lunchtime. Her bottle-blonde hair was dazzling. She would never in a million years get into a hotel in that outfit unless they were hosting a 'Vicars and Tarts' night. Moreover, any bloke whose doorstep she turned up on would have a blue fit – the skirt alone would have every net curtain for miles twitching.

So after we'd established the dress code she relaxed and told me about herself. Marie had three sons: the oldest was 32, the middle one 28, and the youngest 24. She'd been just 14 when she had her first child and from that moment on she had always been responsible for other people, which meant she always came last. And when it wasn't her kids, it was the patients at a nearby hospital where she was a nurse. She had dreams of living in Spain, retiring to the sun without any financial worries. She'd worked all her life, owned a small house in Maidstone and only had the prospect of a tiny pension to subsidise whatever she got from the state when she retired. She wanted a way out. Single and very determined, if anyone was going to realise their dream I was pretty sure that Marie would be the one.

As I had with Jenny, I talked extensively to Marie about the safety and security aspects, which it was essential she followed. Being a nurse, she knew much more about the health issues than I did, and I realised this was not a woman who would take any type of risk. She had first-hand experience of patients with unchecked herpes, gonorrhoea and even syphilis. In fact, until I met her, I hadn't realised quite how dangerous chlamydia could be, and I made a note to pass that information on to my other girls.

Marie wanted to start that night. She had booked a week off work and I think she'd psyched herself up so much that she needed to start right away or she'd lose her nerve. She promised she'd go home and rethink her wardrobe and we said our goodbyes. I headed back home in time to see the kids in from school and start on supper for the evening.

By 6.00 pm that evening, I felt exhausted. I'd been up every night until the two or three in the morning answering the phone and making sure the girls got home all right. Sometimes I managed a nap during the day but usually I just had to make do, and some nights we did finish much earlier if things were quiet. I wasn't complaining – after all, I wasn't working like they were. But the fact was, I could hardly keep my eyes open and I still had another eight hours before I could go to sleep. What I needed was someone to share the phone duty, someone who I could trust enough to do the job properly and without blowing my cover. But who?

Kirsty was an old friend of mine from years back who had recently gone back to college to train as a social worker. I knew she could do with the money so I asked her how she would feel about occasionally taking the calls for me. I had the call divert option put on the phone so she could do it all from her house. Her little ones would be in bed and one or two nights a week I would hand everything over to her. It was a revelation. Instead of rushing to get the children either into bed or settled upstairs with homework, TV or reading, now I was able to take a little more time. I'd spend time chatting with Emily and Alice and we all enjoyed a bit more time together, even if it was just lounging around in front of the telly.

We were all in a routine now. Kirsty took the calls a couple of nights a week. The number of bookings seemed to be steadily increasing and I'd had two more enquiries from girls who wanted to be escorts. We had more clients too, which was fantastic. Tom had rung for Jenny a few times, which was reassuring, and Marie was definitely a hit. She'd had several different clients phone and ask for her again. Importantly for her, she now had the concrete evidence that her escape plan to Spain could become a reality.

The calls from women wanting to join continued and I realised that I needed to be careful not to become too blasé about the business by allowing the list of girls to grow to an unmanageable number or by taking on anyone and everyone who asked to work. After all, I couldn't afford to lose control of what was happening and I needed to be sure that the women who called were all given the same care and consideration I would have expected when I worked. Two incidents really stick in my mind from that time. The first was a meeting with a girl who on the phone had sounded terrific. She wasn't as anxious or nervous as, say, Jenny had been when she called. I arranged to meet her the next day.

I turned up at the appointed time and place and looked around for her. She hadn't arrived so I settled down with the paper. Seconds later a young woman approached me and introduced herself. My first thought was: how did I tell this girl she was too unattractive to be a prostitute? I am sure she was perfectly lovely but she just didn't look the part. Overweight and so badly dressed that I wondered at first if she was having a laugh with me; in fact she was deadly serious. I honestly didn't know what to say but there was little point pretending that we could work together. I simply thanked her for coming to see me and said I'd call her later in the day.

I did find a tactful way out. I told her over the phone that after much deliberation I'd decided that she was too similar to another couple of girls we had at Crystal's so I couldn't give her any work right now, but obviously I'd call her the moment an opening came up.

Call Me Madam

The next girl I met was as different as it was possible to be. Her name was Isobel. She asked if she could meet me at the coffee shop near the station at Rochester. She only had an hour before she had to catch a train back up to London because she was due to work that evening. She was, and indeed still is, an extremely intelligent and lovely looking girl, with English rose skin and long auburn hair. At just 23 years old, Isobel explained how she was recently single and worked full-time for an airline. Her ex, Robbie, was someone she'd met on the first day at university and they'd been together ever since. Until he decided to go off travelling and find himself, that is. Isobel lived in Canterbury in a tiny two-bed flat. She had always been careful with money; she saved for the deposit and her parents had surprised her and given her some money on her 21st birthday so she'd gone ahead and bought the flat with assurances from Robbie that he would be around forever – they were engaged after all, weren't they? He had not bought the flat with her because he was between jobs at the time, and they would rectify that when he had established himself in his new job. He was a graphic artist, quite a good one too, but there were loads of good graphic artists floating about.

Isobel had taken languages at university but really had no idea what she really wanted to do and had just drifted into the position with the airline. Her German was really quite good, and she did enjoy the job. The shifts played havoc with her social life, but in compensation the time off was great. After working with the airline for a year, she'd decided that what she really wanted was to qualify as a secondary-school teacher. Having discussed it with

81

Robbie, who had by now started a new job, they agreed she should go part-time at work and attempt to gain her PGCE teaching certificate as a part-time student. Robbie was happy at first; he paid the mortgage and Isobel paid what she could – after all it was their future she was investing in.

Until, that is, Robbie decided to go. And he did just that, upped and left. Isobel came home from a late shift and the flat was completely devoid of any of his belongings. Just a note, 'Sorry, R x', and that was their relationship summed up – the last eight years of her life condensed into one word, an initial and a solitary kiss.

Heartbroken didn't come into it. Devastated, then angry, next came bewildered, until inevitably, practical. Isobel's income was minuscule compared with the outgoings she had. She thought about finding a lodger but that wouldn't be enough, and it would be such a waste not to finish the course now; she was only nine months from being a fully qualified teacher. Options spun around in her head – maybe her parents would help, the bank perhaps – but she knew that once she was in debt, trying to pull herself out would take forever. She had never been in debt in her life and had no intention of doing so now, all because of that spineless wonder. The ad for the escort agency practically screamed at her as she flicked through the local paper after enjoying one of her mum's vast Sunday lunches. She quizzed herself as she drove home that evening, the 'Could I . . . ?' and the 'Should I . . . ?' all mixed up with morality, necessity and the strong desire to stand on her own two feet.

By the time she got home she had decided to take a chance. She told me that the ad for Crystal's didn't look quite as salacious as some of the others she'd seen, which was what had prompted the call, even though, as she had discovered, the logistics of managing her day job and her degree course along with an escorting job was going to mean she'd have to be a genius at diary management. I kept on about how exhausting the work would be and how you had to be so nice, so terribly nice, to everyone. I didn't stand a chance of dissuading her though.

Isobel was the queen of being nice to people – it was what she did at work all day long. She started working for me the following week, using a pre-arranged holiday from work. That first week she worked three nights, and slept and studied the rest of the time. The money Isobel earned was way beyond her expectations and obviously she was over the moon about this. But I worried whether she would know when to stop. That she, and some of the other girls too, would not see the work just as a short-term solution to the problems they had from lack of money. The euphoria of banking the money you've made from a night's work is all well and good, but once those bills are paid, once the arrears are resolved, you have to walk away, because trying to live with the demons of being a prostitute is far from easy.

Chapter Six

*T*he day of Victoria's hospital appointment had finally arrived. I picked Paul up and we took a train to Victoria Station, then a cab over to the Royal Brompton. Victoria was so excited by the whole experience and insisted on sitting on (and off!) the taxi's tip-up seat, her little hand gripping the armrest and her face pressed up against the window. It was a cold and crisp spring day, when London looks its best. My little girl didn't seem in the least bit worried; nothing could spoil the pleasure for her of having a day off school and the promise of somewhere nice for lunch afterwards. As I leaned back in the taxi, I felt the strain of the last years coming flooding back. In spite of the fact that the business was doing well and that so far nothing much had gone wrong, I couldn't help feeling a bit anxious as I tried to juggle home and work. Paul hardly spoke as the taxi weaved in and out of the heavy traffic. We had so little to say to one another. I wondered if he ever questioned how we were managing financially as he certainly never tried to find out. Perhaps he was afraid I might ask for help. In some ways I resented Paul. He never even bothered to ask how I managed, how I held everything together – perhaps he was just scared of the answer. Maybe he knew what I was doing; maybe he didn't bother to ask because by asking the question he would be acknowledging his own inadequacies as a provider for his children.

Eventually we arrived at the hospital and went upstairs to the clinic. I gave Victoria's details to the receptionist and we were sent off for her ECG, which again she thought was terribly exciting. Whilst we waited our turn, Victoria played with the toys and books in the children's corner. I think I had a lump in my throat the whole time we were there. There were so many children with so many problems, yet they all seemed oblivious to the soaring emotions of their parents. Victoria was called in to see Dr Astley, a leading specialist in electrical heart problems in children. Dr Astley could obviously sense my anxiety as she looked at Victoria's results and read through her patient notes. As she began to speak to me, the tears started to well in my eyes. She must have seen it a thousand times before – desperate, haunted parents, so frightened of what they might hear that they can hardly take in the information they're being given, irrespective of whether it's good or bad. That was me. It must have been obvious that I was barely able to register what she was saying, so instead she turned her attention to Victoria and played with her until I'd managed to compose myself enough to listen. Paul sat next to me, impassive, probably going through the same emotions but just not able to express them.

Victoria told the doctor about the butterflies and how she had been watching TV and felt funny. Dr Astley listened to Victoria's heart and let Victoria listen too, which she found curiously amusing. Then she gave me a monitor, which she explained would need to be attached to Victoria with electrodes for the next two weeks. She showed me how to take the readings and told me to send them down the telephone line back to the hospital. The machine would pick up any irregularities and show exactly what was happening. Until she had seen the readings, the doctor couldn't say whether Victoria's condition was cause for concern or just required careful monitoring.

The jumble of feelings was painful. I was relieved, anxious, tearful and scared all at once. We left and made our way out into the spring sunshine and found an Italian restaurant where Victoria was spoilt rotten by the waiters and had a lovely time. I watched her, played with her and tried to act normal, but inside my mind sobbed silent tears for my baby and her uncertain future.

Chapter Seven

*T*he guy sitting before me was an Adonis, a fully-fledged Adonis. The word stayed a permanent fixture in my mind as I chatted to the gorgeous fireman. He looked at me, with his sapphire blue eyes, which were framed with black lashes – the length and lustre of which any woman would kill for – and contemplated his answers to my questions.

He looked perfectly normal yet abnormally perfect, and I was blushing like a schoolgirl. I tried my best to stay composed as he comfortably told me, 'Oh yes, I like to receive as well as give . . .' and it took me a moment to catch on to what he was saying, '. . . couples . . . whatever, really.'

'Oh, good, that's good, really good,' was my totally inadequate, pathetic response.

I had finally found some time to interview a few potential male escorts, but having this sort of conversation on a serious and professional level was making me feel incredibly bashful, coy even. God knows how colourful my life had been, but I really was having trouble discussing these things with such a beautiful, perfect man. But once he started talking about the price of polyurethane condoms all my images of his perfection crumbled away. Oh well, I thought, I guess I'll stick to David after all.

And so it came to pass that gorgeous, beautiful god-like Ritchie became the first male employee of Crystal Escorts. As he was a local fireman he had plenty of spare time on his hands. Excellent, I thought, he's already got the gear to cater for one of the most popular female fantasies.

Ritchie had tried all the usual types of part-time employment to make some extra money, and had evidently found pall-bearing and paramedic call-out far too tame, much to my amusement. Requests had come in for all types of weird and wonderful combinations of sexes and participants, so I thought that having a man on the books would enable the agency to branch out, as it were. Why I felt so coy about dealing with Richie I have no idea. I suppose it's one thing to have graphic, matter-of-fact conversations about sex with clients or other women and quite another to have them with a prospective employee. Ridiculous but true.

The following Monday morning the office phone rang and I automatically answered it, even though our ad clearly said that we opened at 7.00 pm. It was a woman who introduced herself as Lucy. She was speaking so quietly, virtually whispering, and explained that she was at work at the moment so talking was clearly difficult, but she'd seen the ad and was very interested in finding out more. Obviously I realised it would be very difficult for me to get more than a 'Yes' or a 'No' to my questions, so we arranged to meet in a sandwich bar in Chatham that lunchtime near where she worked, which made a nice change from the local wine bar.

I arrived first, found a table and ordered a coffee. A slim, petite, gorgeous girl with long curly hair, aged about 25, came over and asked if I was Dawn. She held her hand out confidently as she introduced herself. Lucy told me how she was so glad she had seen my ad because it could really help her. She was stunning, confident and articulate. Lucy was married to a sailor in the Royal Navy who worked away for much of the time. She didn't have any kids, which left me rather puzzled as to what her motives were. She was nicely dressed and certainly didn't give the impression that she was wanting financially. It was only when Lucy started to talk about wanting a new conservatory and this fabulous fireplace she had seen that I began to get the picture. I couldn't believe she was willing to take this enormous risk just for inanimate objects. Not for kids, or paying the mortgage but for a marble fireplace! I stopped her mid-spiel and brought forward one of my standard questions, 'You do realise you'll have to sleep with strangers, have sex with them?'

'Of course!' she laughed.

Was I missing something here? I could just about comprehend why addicts became prostitutes, and indeed why every other woman who was working with me was doing it, but Lucy I had absolutely no understanding of at all. On the one hand, having Lucy work for Crystal's would increase our bookings, of that I had no doubt. But on the other, was it really right for me to give her the opportunity to expose herself to this sort of life? It was clear that she wasn't stupid, and nor was she being coerced into anything, but was I guilty purely by providing the opportunity? Yet Lucy was determined that this was a path she was going to take. And as much as I felt shocked – stunned even – that she was willing to become a prostitute purely for those luxurious extras, I knew that if I said no to her, she would go elsewhere. At least if she worked through Crystal Escorts she would be as safe as possible, and I decided to say yes to her as it seemed the lesser of two evils.

Meeting Lucy and listening to her flippancy was a turning point for me in understanding human nature. As time went by and her true motives revealed themselves, I felt humbled over my first impressions of Lucy and my reaction to her reasons for becoming an escort. I did eventually come across one woman who wanted to work with me as an escort for no other conceivable reason other than the money, even proudly telling me about her wardrobe that was full of designer clothes and handbags. By that time I'd come to realise that the world is definitely made up of all types of people and nothing surprised me any more. It saddened me, but I wasn't shocked. The only saving grace was that this woman was pretty much in the minority – the other escorts were only doing it because they really believed there was no other way.

Lucy asked me if I thought she was attractive enough for the work and if she was suitable. I remember wondering the self-same thing as I looked at the ad that changed my life several years and many experiences ago. I assured her she most definitely was and asked her if she had rung any other agencies. She said she had, but didn't like the idea of dealing with a mobile number, which seemed to be the norm for the others. She felt there was no base, that she couldn't imagine an office behind these mobile numbers or any precautions for safety. It was as if their only interest was their fee. The other agencies also seemed to be run by men, which also made her feel vulnerable. From her comments, I could see that Lucy had obviously thought about her decision very carefully, over some time. She had watched the ad appear every week, in several newspapers, and always with a landline phone number. I asked her to think hard, to seriously think it through – the double life, the lies, the explanations as to where the extra money was coming from and, most importantly, the risks involved. There was also the diseases, the danger, the risk of discovery and the impact that it would have on her life. Her answers kicked down every barrier I put up, and I told her I would call her later. She said she hoped I would take her on because, if not, her only other option was to place her own ad. I was horrified for her – horrified at just how vulnerable she would be. It wasn't my place to try to play mother and protector to all these women but I really did feel responsible, because it was through my ad that they were exposed to the reality of making money this way. Of course that was ridiculous, especially bearing in mind that I had only just met Lucy, but it's how I felt deep down.

Anyway, off she went, back to her office job at the local council offices, oblivious to the true cost to her soul of that new conservatory. I called Lucy later that evening and told her she could start whenever she felt she was ready. We talked about the practical side of things such as which road atlas and condoms to buy, which nights she could work, exactly what she should wear, how to pay her fees, and that was it – done. Lucy wanted to get started right away and joked about hoping she was busy because she had just signed up for the finance on the conservatory. I shook my head at the phone in disbelief.

Lucy turned out to be the consummate professional; nothing seemed to faze her. Halfway through her second week I had a call from a client in Gillingham. Alan was a black guy with a stunning body. I'd been to him myself a couple of years ago, and have to admit that it wasn't an altogether unpleasant experience. Alan wanted a couple and wondered if that was a service Crystal's could provide. Somehow, rather stupidly, that had not really occurred to me – I had requests from men wanting a man but a man wanting a couple – could I do that? I was very conscious of the pressure I'd been under when I worked for Holly's agency. I had never felt able to say no to a booking because I was worried it might be looked upon unfavourably, that I'd then be passed over for future work. I wanted the girls to be comfortable with telling me they really didn't want to do a threesome, or whatever it was, if it wasn't their scene.

I asked Lucy if she wanted to do it. I reassured her that she shouldn't feel she had to take the booking – no one was pushing anyone into doing anything they weren't comfortable with. But she was keen to go ahead, as was Ritchie. I rang Alan with the good news, and he happily accepted my price, each escort getting their usual individual fee. I arranged for Lucy and Ritchie to meet up about 20 minutes before they were due at Alan's house. That in itself was weird – they had never met before and were about to have sex in front of, and with, another man! I told them to meet in a car park near the booking, which they did. As they drove to Alan's they discussed how far they were each prepared to go. I was really concerned that Lucy was happy about this and felt I was somehow crossing a line. Actually, she seemed to genuinely enjoy what she was doing, and it had to be said that both Alan and Ritchie had gorgeous bodies. I checked in with Lucy a couple of times during the booking and she assured me she felt safe and in control. We'd even devised a 'safe' word in case she was ever in any bother, as I did with all of the girls. I had been in unusual situations many times myself, but that didn't mean I felt comfortable about putting someone else in that position.

Chapter Eight

Victoria had worn the monitor for the prescribed two-week period and I'd plugged the device into the phone each night and sent the readings back to the hospital. The butterflies had continued with alarming regularity but I felt that something was at least being done about the episode. Nevertheless I was still worried out of my mind about her. As the doctor had suggested, Victoria continued as normal with her sports and activities at school, slightly fed up at having to wear the monitor and the marks it was leaving on her chest and back, but other than that neither the monitor nor having the palpitations seemed to bother her a great deal.

An appointment had been arranged for the following week so Victoria, Paul and I repeated our journey and went back to the Royal Brompton Hospital. The readings showed that Victoria was having palpitations – her heart was skipping beats and then accelerating at a ridiculously high level. It wasn't painful for her, just uncomfortable and it left her breathless. A nurse supervised whilst Victoria played a game with a toddler and I sat opposite Dr Astley listening to her analysis of the readings and the latest ECG. She wanted to find out exactly which part of Victoria's heart the problem was originating from because she felt it was dangerous for Victoria to continue having this number of palpitations. In the meantime, she prescribed some beta blockers for Victoria to take every day and said arrangements would be made for an operation to find out exactly where the damage to her heart was. We were to take Victoria over to the children's ward for some blood tests and Dr Astley would be in touch shortly.

When I looked around the ward and saw the other children, things slid into perspective just fractionally – at least they knew what was wrong with my baby and the prescribed medicine would go some way towards making her 'better'. What about all these children? Some had no hair, one little girl was in a wheelchair with an oxygen tank attached to her nostrils. How on earth did their parents cope? My heart was breaking for each and every one of these kids. A little girl with no hair and no eyebrows played Connect 4 with Victoria whilst a blood sample was taken, and I'd never felt so useless or humble in my life.

Chapter Nine

March 9th was my 35th birthday and a big group of us went out for dinner to my favourite restaurant in Rochester. As Kirsty, my dear friend and now trusted telephonist, was coming out for dinner with us, I asked an old friend who had been such a support to me when I was escorting to answer the phone for the evening. Over the years, Sarah had looked after the children, supported my decision to become an escort and hidden my suitcase of working clothes in her garage. In the early days she had always known where I was going and what I was doing, just in case. She had been such a great help both emotionally and practically and now, here she was again, helping me with Crystal's. Sarah had a wonderful sense of humour and dealt with the crank calls with such finesse. She called herself 'Gloria' and I think some clients phoned just to chat to her. She'd been taking the calls for me once a week for a few weeks now, as well as Kirsty doing a couple of nights a week, because I was finding that we were still taking bookings at 2.00 or 3.00 am, and by the time the girls were coming out of the last job it was four in the morning or even later. As the kids were getting up for school at 7.00 am, three hours sleep left me pretty washed out and, despite sometimes going back to bed once I had dropped them off, it was never the same.

Christina had phoned me earlier in the day to let me know she had a booking of her own at 9.30 pm but would be available either side of that. I nagged her about safety again – it was something that I just had to keep hammering home after the things that had happened to me in my previous incarnation as an escort. She told me to stop worrying and to enjoy my birthday, and she'd see me tomorrow.

The next morning I made my weekly call to the ever-helpful Daphne at the paper, to check my advertisements were all set to run as usual. She mentioned that Christina had not been in to pay for her own ad, which she always did, 9.00 am on the nail, in person, in cash. Daphne knew that Christina also worked with me and asked if she was okay. My next call was to Christina – no reply, so I left a quick message.

I was peeling some potatoes for dinner when the doorbell rang and, glancing at the clock, I flicked on the kettle, expecting it to be my favourite battleaxe breezing in. Indeed it was, but, for the first time ever, with no wind in her sails and every ounce of life sapped from her face. She stood there and silently pulled down the pashmina, which she had draped over her hair and shoulders.

As she turned to face me, I saw the bruises across her face, then came the silent tears and she clung to me for dear life.

'Jesus, Christina, what's happened? Who's done this to you?'

'Don't,' she responded. 'Just don't say you warned me.'

We sat for what seemed like hours at my kitchen table, Christina's hands cradling a cup of coffee laced with a shot of brandy. At first, she'd hardly said a word, just the address, which was all the explanation I needed. As her story continued, it was all so bloody familiar. I knew it word for word because the same thing had happened to me. And until then, I hadn't even been able to talk about it. Even now I hate to recount what happened.

Around two years ago I'd taken a phone call from Holly in the early afternoon. She gave me an 8.00 pm booking for that evening and, great bonus, it turned out to be only about 20 minutes drive away. That was to be my first booking of the evening so I had longer with the kids and time to plough through the ironing. At 7.30 pm I was changed, ready, had said goodnight to the kids and babysitter, and was about to leave. I did the usual handbag check, though for slightly unusual contents – condoms, money, keys, vibrator, notepad, pen, map book, make-up, baby wipes – all present and correct, and off I went. The click of the central locking started my evening, as I then drove to the address, a rather shabby-looking ground-floor maisonette in Rainham.

I stood at the front door of the house and checked that it was the correct flat before pushing the doorbell. A voice came out on the intercom and told me to come on in – the door to the flat was open and just to close it behind me. I walked through the communal hallway and to the front door of the flat, which was slightly open. I should have known better than to walk through the door to a home without first seeing who was in it – I can't believe I was so stupid. Yet, I did what I was told. I was about to turn around to shut the door behind me when I saw him, lurking behind the door. I didn't stand a chance – he was at least 6'3" and he towered over me, leaning into my face. He grabbed me and backed me into the door with such force it slammed shut behind me. Trying desperately to retain my composure, I looked at the man standing before me. He was hideous, dressed as a woman, complete with grotesque make-up. He wore a long black wig, black fishnet stockings and high heels, a black bra over false plastic breasts and a mini-skirt. Still pinning me to the door, he leaned across me and slid the top bolt and turned the key before pulling it out of the lock. I couldn't get out now, so he released me and as he teetered across the room in his heels, I could see his penis dangling below the hem of his skirt.

Scared out of my mind, I was literally rooted to the spot – I couldn't move, couldn't scream or do anything as he stood surveying me, one hand on his hip, whilst touching himself with the other. He came towards me, grabbed me by the arm and pulled me to the ground, sneering at me.

'You think you're so fucking special, don't you, but you're just a fucking whore like the rest of them, nothing but a whore like the rest of them, nothing but a whore, a cunt for sale.'

I knew there was no use in fighting him, he was far too strong for me and as he kept up his revolting monologue of abuse, he pulled my clothes aside and penetrated me, holding me down as I sobbed. When he had satisfied himself he released his grip on me and I realised with horror that he hadn't used a condom. Despite the terror of the situation and the immediate physical threat to my life, my mind reverted to the regimen of sexual health I had drummed into it. I suppose it was a way of blocking out one fear with another.

Now he was done with me, he methodically unlocked and opened the door. He picked up my bag, throwing it and me out of the room, followed by obscenity after obscenity, as if somehow I'd been the cause of it all. I stumbled to the sanctuary of my car, fumbling until I somehow pushed the central locking control and locked myself in. Sobbing, gasping for breath, hardly able to see through my tears, I drove away, pulling up after about five minutes as the shaking was so bad I felt unable to control the car. I could still feel him all over me, the pressure of his body on top of me, pushing and hurting me, the legacy of the appalling act still within me. I opened the car door and vomited, then sobbed.

Christina showed me the other marks on her body – she had suffered more than I had at the hands of this maniac – and gradually told me what had happened. Our experiences were very similar, although he had been more violent towards her because she had tried to fight back. Christina is not usually very affectionate; she's the sort of person with whom one would never do anything more than the occasional air kiss, but she melted when I put my hand over hers.

Anger only just holding off the tears, Christina said, 'Why didn't I take any notice of you?'

'Christina, love, it doesn't matter now. It's over, you're safe, so don't be hard on yourself.'

She was totally devastated, as if every ounce of fight had left her. I held her hand as she cried quiet tears, trying to offer words of comfort and pleading with her to stop working, to go back to looking for a job in the City – surely nothing was worth this? Christina wiped her face and explained that she just had to carry on and, despite wishing so desperately that she felt differently, I said I understood.

'But, please,' I bargained, 'no more ads. Just work with me and then I'll know where you are.'

Trying not to cry again, stunned at the effect the experience had had on her, Christina agreed. I think that perhaps her own belief in herself had been so immense that she was shocked to the very core of her being that anyone would ever have the audacity to upset her world.

She agreed, no more ads, and caution became her middle name. I told Sarah and Kirsty what had happened but all we could do was be aware that the address was most definitely out of bounds. I could have called the police, and I have no doubt that they would have taken the call very seriously but for the fact that Christina was working as a prostitute, and any defence barrister would have had a field day with her and the media would let the whole world know what she did for a living. We just had to carry on as usual.

Although Christina's body healed fairly quickly – after only a few days she had no visible marks – the emotional scars that no one but she and I knew about would take much longer. I knew from experience that they would fade in time; they'd never completely heal but they would fade. She took the rest of the week off and never did place another ad with Daphne. Her dreadful experience was a reminder again that being an escort was a dangerous profession and that for all the decent men out there, there's always someone, somewhere, just waiting to take out his hatred of women on some poor unsuspecting girl.

The same night Christina suffered her appalling experience Jenny had an all-night booking with a client she'd seen before. I was glad for her that it was working out so well. It's not often you get booked for the whole night, and most girls are delighted when it happens. Of course, there are times when it can be a nightmare, either because the guy is revolting or weird or, as often is the case, because he's decided to snort a load of cocaine and is therefore up for a non-stop four-hour session of exhausting sex. All the girls knew that if at any time things weren't working out, they could walk. Luckily for Jenny, she was off to a rather nice part of the world – Sevenoaks – to see Andrew. But there was something about the booking that was worrying me, though I didn't tell her. When I'd called her earlier that evening to let her know, Jenny sounded genuinely pleased that Andrew had booked her again. I asked her if she would be okay for an overnight and she reassured me that her sister had agreed to stay over and babysit. The last time she'd seen him, she'd mentioned to me afterwards what a dish this Andrew was. Now, on the phone, I could tell as I was giving her the details that she had floated off into another world, her voice taking on that dreamy quality which could only mean one thing. She'd fallen for him.

When she called me the following morning to let me know all was well, I suggested she popped in later for a cup of tea and a catch-up, before she picked up her little boy from playschool. Jenny stood at my front door with a beautiful smile on her face, looking totally gorgeous. I hadn't seen her for a couple of weeks, but even in that short space of time the difference was amazing. She had lost a little weight and bought some new clothes. How different she looked from when we first met. Now she exuded confidence. I made tea and said, as casually as I could, 'So, tell me about Andrew.'

Jenny didn't even try to hide the fact that she was absolutely smitten. She told me how when he'd first opened the door to her, she'd been so surprised to see that he was as gorgeous as she remembered. Andrew did something in the City, he had explained to Jenny – nothing terribly exciting, he just moved money around and it sort of turned into more money. Jenny didn't really understand what he was talking about and, the way he explained it, it sounded like he found it very boring anyway. She described his flat to me: hi-tech and minimal with shiny surfaces. No little fingerprints on the walls or Lego or Sticklebricks spilling out of plastic storage boxes like in her lounge.

Jenny had been tongue-tied on her first booking with him because Andrew was so posh. He was very public school; she, as she liked to put it, was very state secondary. He'd told her that he was lonely; he didn't have a girlfriend and was really quite shy. He said he couldn't stand all that pretentious crap that passed for conversation in the wine bars his friends frequented. Andrew admitted to going to massage parlours on stag nights with his friends, but had never actually called an agency before. Of course some of the guys at work talked about their exploits with girls from agencies, tall stories of coked-out bimbos. But – and Jenny looked embarrassed as she told me this – Andrew had said she was definitely not what he had expected at all. Jenny had been around, and had grown up on the Denton estate, which translated to a hard upbringing – of that there was no question. She'd had that second booking with him and I could see her imagining herself as Julia Roberts, Andrew as Richard Gere. I knew what would come next. She would give him her mobile number and he would take her out to dinner, somewhere he would be sure not to bump into any of his 'circle' and they'd end up back at his place for the night with her refusing his offer of payment.

Just like clockwork, Andrew rang later that day and confirmed another overnight booking for Jenny. Knowing the bubble would likely burst very soon, I tried to soften the blow a little for her by way of financial compensation. I told him I'd had several other requests for her that evening so he would have to pay her the full, pro-rata rate. I plucked an extortionate figure out of the air and he didn't turn a hair. I said it had to be cash too, as we didn't take cheques. This was not strictly true, but I had witnessed too many times a client gain a girl's confidence until she was blasé about the payment. Fine, no problem at all, he said. The night came and went without a hitch. Jenny had earned a great deal of money, but some days later the inevitable call from Andrew came. Did I have anyone else available, someone quite different from Jenny?

I couldn't tell her, so when she asked if he'd called, I said no. Finally, she came to see me. Anxiety was etched all over her face, and she looked tired, emotionally tired. Was I sure he hadn't rung? Perhaps she'd been on another booking? No, love, sorry I told her, trying to make light of it, you know the golden rule, don't ever fall for a client. Yes, she agreed, it really wasn't a good idea. She had only met him a few times but because of her vulnerability and her overwhelming desire to be lifted out of all this by a knight in shining armour, she was terribly, terribly hurt by what she saw as his rejection of her. All Jenny wanted was to be loved – how well I'd known that feeling . . .

Since the beginning of March and all through April the number of bookings had been increasing on a weekly basis. The jobs seemed to be distributed fairly evenly between the girls and Ritchie was called upon once a week at least. Everyone was reliable, punctual and finding their way around Kent without too much trouble. The number of regular clients was increasing and we were all in a stable routine.

By now I had become firm friends with a girl called Sharon, who was also on the books. Sharon was 38 and from Newcastle – she had the thickest Geordie accent I have ever heard. Sharon was the mother of four young kids and wife to a deadbeat third husband, who had spent his time sponging off her and sleeping around. By the time she had finally had enough and kicked him out, the bills were starting to mount in a scary fashion. Though she was working full-time selling advertising space, it just wasn't enough, and she contacted me out of sheer desperation. Sharon was attractive but sad and lonely like most of the women who worked for me. Unfortunately, she was just another all-too-common statistic: a lone mum who single-handedly had to provide for her kids.

One regular client was Colin, and he liked to see Sharon. She hadn't said much about him, her only comment being a loud groan when he booked her for the second time. One evening, Kirsty was taking the calls whilst Sharon and I were sitting in a restaurant in Rochester having a fabulous Thai meal. Sharon was going to work later; she had a booking for 11.00 pm so we had taken the opportunity to have a catch-up. I persuaded her to tell me about Colin and she did so, hesitantly at first.

'Oh you know, nothing to tell really, he's a van driver, he often goes to Europe.'

'But . . .' I continued for her.

'Saying this I really hate myself for feeling this way, but he gives me the creeps and it's so not his fault. He's disabled; one leg is about four inches shorter than the other and, it's not just that, but the house is just so filthy . . . I just don't know if I can do it any more, see him I mean. And you know how I've been going about three times a week? Well, he's started to write me love letters and he wants to marry me.'

Jenny's situation reversed. Obsessed clients are a nightmare. They fantasise that they are actually having a relationship with you, that somehow you are their girlfriend and have real feelings for them. This had happened to me in the past, and it was very tempting to take the easy path and take advantage of the situation. Sharon was in a dilemma. She was earning a lot of money from Colin and he was also giving her presents – a bottle of perfume here and there, a top-up card for her phone, even a silver bracelet on one occasion. But she couldn't stand him and made every excuse to get out of the bookings as quickly as possible. I couldn't really blame her; it was horrible having to be intimate with someone who made you feel sick. It wasn't just a physical thing, she explained. It was him as a person. From what he'd told her, Colin had not had a real relationship with a woman before and the basic things that should have been obvious seemed to have been overlooked.

Sharon had me in stitches as she described how dirty the house was and how one night she had spent the two hours he'd booked cleaning the bedroom, washing the sheets and even going to Asda to buy a new duvet – because she'd told him there was no way she was going to endure that filth again. Colin unfortunately seemed to be interpreting Sharon's attempt to make her visits to the house a little more bearable as more of a nest-building thing. I did feel wicked, laughing as Sharon described how she'd made him have a shower and shouted instructions, like 'Use more soap!' and 'Scrub the bottoms of your feet!'

The trouble was that, as Colin probably saw it, Sharon was obviously interested in him because she'd got involved in a hands-on way in his housekeeping. Well, I hoped to God she was prepared for the potential consequences. Everything Christina believed had taken a huge battering and she was a different person after the attack. Jenny had dared for a moment to dream of another life and, despite being let down, her new-found aspirations for a better future would give her the confidence to make that happen. Being an escort opens your eyes and your heart. Like it or not, you gain a greater knowledge of yourself, as these women were just beginning to discover.

Chapter Ten

*B*y the middle of May, several more women had taken the enormous step of picking up the phone and calling Crystal Escorts to ask for work. In fact there were now two male escorts and 15 ladies on the agency's books. Despite all my personal experience as an escort, the stories they recounted still fascinated me.

If a client wanted something a little out of the ordinary he would almost always say beforehand. The girls were all consenting adults and were never under any pressure to go back to a client when they didn't want to, or to stay if things developed in a way they weren't comfortable with. The way it generally worked was that an escort would visit a client and the booking would just proceed in the normal way. If the client felt comfortable with the girl and wanted something a little more, shall we say, 'adventurous', a serious discussion would ensue. If both parties were happy, then the guy would give the girl a detailed indication of exactly what it was he was looking for.

Sharon visited a chap in Tunbridge Wells who liked a little bit of extra excitement. He always rang and made the booking at least a day in advance to check that Sharon was available and give her time to prepare. She needed to bring a change of clothes – the black latex variety – and a couple of pieces of equipment. Put simply, he liked to be spanked with various canes, whips and paddles whilst having a variety of objects pushed into his anus. After several visits, this guy had given Sharon the money to buy the things he required. Regardless of what was about to occur, you would never have known these girls were escorts had you bumped into them in a hotel foyer or a wine bar, because they were just smartly dressed women, no hint of anything risqué. Certainly no PVC or thigh-high boots on display. Of course, the contents of the bag of tricks they might carry with them would have turned a few heads.

I called Marie for our usual Monday morning catch-up at about 11.00 am and she immediately launched into an excited babble. 'I have been desperate for you to ring! You'll never believe what happened to me! Oh my God, and he paid me extra to do it!' Eventually, when she had stopped giggling and calmed down, Marie told me that she'd been to a booking with Brian, a regular client of the agency; she'd been to visit him a couple of times now. Brian was apparently a well-built, very well-endowed guy, about 30 years old. Marie started to giggle again as she described her first visit. He had sat in the bath and asked her to stand with her feet on either edge, straddling him, then pee all over him! And that was it, no sex; he just masturbated whilst she did it. But this Saturday night had been even more bizarre – he had produced a jug and asked Marie to pee in it. Brian proceeded once again to climb into the bath, only this time he drank her pee as she poured it into his mouth, whilst obliging him with a hand job. I wondered how she managed to do both at the same time. I also wondered how a guy worked out that something like that turned him on!

I guess some people are just more sexually curious than others, and through experimentation find new things that turn them on. As we all became aware of the variety of sexual interests our clients had, I think we became less and less judgemental. Where was the harm in a man wanting anal stimulation? What was so wrong with being peed on? As long as those taking part are consenting adults and it's done in private, they're harmless acts. Granted, they might be different from the norm, but the stigma of the word 'perverted' seems unfair. The only place I could find perversion was where there was a lack of consent.

A problem I was encountering more and more was that many of the girls had no one else to talk to except me. So as well as the many other roles in my jam-packed life, I was a confessional, a counsellor and general receiver of woe/happiness/amazement. When I was working, I had a couple of very close friends to whom I disclosed my secret life, and in time was so grateful to have these trusted friends to turn to for sanctuary and counselling, as well as for more practical help. Obviously that involved a huge amount of trust and integrity on their part, and I soon realised that some of the girls of Crystal Escorts had no one to whom they felt comfortable revealing the truth about their double lives. The work carried with it a huge emotional and psychological impact so it fell to me to be their punchbag. Part and parcel of the job, I concluded. But it was becoming increasingly hard to detach myself from the agency on the days I wasn't working, and I felt such divided loyalties. On the one hand I wanted to be there for the girls, but when I was trying to do something with the kids and give them my attention, it was a hard juggling act.

In amongst the various obsessions and crazy people we dealt with, there was one incident that was particularly disturbing and, in some ways, marked a major turning point for me as it put me on the radar of the authorities.

Isobel had a booking with a new client, and as everything checked out and I had no particular misgivings, I just went through the usual precautions. She called as normal when she arrived at the booking; just under an hour later, my phone rang again and Isobel started talking so fast that I had to slow her down so I could take it all in. This man, let's call him Peter, obviously found Isobel very attractive and had decided to share his fantasies with her. He had started off stroking her legs and complimenting her on her slim physique and youthfulness. He told her how much he loved children, how he liked to go to the park and watch the children, how he especially liked to see the short white socks and the very young girls in the summer when they walked home from school in their short skirts, and so his descriptions went on. Isobel said she was petrified but didn't want to spook him in case he became violent, so she let him continue. He told her he had things, images of little girls, of children being abused. He asked her to give him a blow-job without taking off her clothes, and she did what he wanted, trying to take as much in about the house as she possibly could. Brave girl, to see it through, knowing all this. As soon as she could, she left, and phoned me.

I was really shocked. What if that same creep had watched one of my children playing in the park? What if he'd developed a thing for Deborah or Victoria? After all, they often went to the park with one of the older girls. I knew I was going to have to phone the police but it was the last thing I wanted to do. After all, what on earth was I going to say? 'Hello, it's Dawn Annandale. I run an escort agency and one of the girls has just given a blow-job to someone she thinks might be a paedophile?'

It worried me all night. What if they shut me down? What if I was given a criminal record? I was so terrified but, in the end, I just knew that I would not be able to live with my conscience if I didn't alert the police. Memories of the abuse I had suffered flooded through me, as if it were yesterday. Without another second's hesitation, I dialled Chatham Police Station and asked to be put through to someone who could deal with a suspected sex offender, though I didn't know how on earth I was going to explain my story. The switchboard told me they were putting me through to someone in CID. I knew the abbreviation from *The Bill*, but that was about it.

A friendly voice answered and I started to stumble over my words. I guess the man at the other end was used to dealing with people who are trying to say something but don't have a clue how to say it. He was very patient with me and told me to just take my time. I explained that I ran an escort agency and wanted to tell him something about a client who had seen one of the girls who worked with me. He asked me my name, just my first name, and then suggested that it might be easier if we met in person. I was a bit taken aback by this, but agreed, assuming he'd want me to go down to the police station. In fact, to my surprise, the officer suggested we met for coffee in Hempstead Valley Shopping Centre the following day.

I was about 20 minutes early for the meeting so I ordered a double espresso and opened the book I had brought with me. I was so nervous I couldn't concentrate at all on the words on the page, which was just as well because a few minutes later a tired, unshaven man in his mid-30s sat in the chair opposite me, put his cappuccino on the table and tightly smiled a hello. He didn't look like anyone from *The Bill*. In fact I was just about to say, sorry but I'm waiting for someone when he put his hand out and said, 'Hi, Dawn, I'm Tony.' He leaned forward and spoke quietly: yes, of course he knew who *I* was, that I ran Crystal Escorts. I felt completely spooked and overwhelmed by this information but it got worse. He said I had even been followed from home this morning to make sure I turned up. After all, it wasn't often that 'someone like me' willingly gave the police information about their punters. I was suddenly no longer nervous, just plain angry. Did this mean that my house was being watched? I stopped him right there, telling Tony not to get ahead of himself and also asking him what the hell he meant by 'someone like me'. What was he trying to do, upset me from the word go? I'd taken the trouble to give the police valuable information – the kind of information that could genuinely, if they could be bothered to follow it up, save some little girl from a horrendous ordeal – and he was using the meeting to make sneering suggestions about 'my sort.' Tony looked at me, full of contempt.

'Come on, love, you know what I mean, you being a prozzy, not exactly the most reliable source, are you?'

Now I was absolutely furious and told Tony he was doing a good job of alienating the one person who was trying to help him here. As far as I was concerned, nothing was more important than the safety of children and that was the only time I would ever come running to the 'boys in blue'. Now, did he want to listen or did he want to sit there with a smug grin on his face in an attempt to scare me? Tony gestured to another man at a nearby table who introduced himself politely as Ray. It was immediately apparent that Ray had much nicer manners than Tony, whom I then proceeded to ignore.

I told Ray exactly what had happened and, without mentioning any names, how frightened Isobel had been. I handed over Peter's phone number and address – the rest was up to them. I hadn't touched my coffee but didn't feel like hanging around to chat so I told Ray that if I ever found out I was being watched I would be in touch, but would he please now back off and let me carry on my legitimate business.

I had tried to do the right thing because of the information I had and this man, Tony, was treating me like some kind of leper. Maybe in his line of work Tony was so used to seeing the bad in people that he was naturally cynical. Maybe he was just tired of the prostitutes he normally dealt with, the streetwalkers with a habit, and he was lumping us all together, refusing to differentiate between feeding a habit and feeding your family. Ray pushed a piece of paper with a mobile number on it into my hand, just like in every cheesy cop show. Never planning to use it, I stuffed it into my handbag and headed home, scared out of my mind at the world I had just walked into. The whole episode made me shudder at the vulnerability of our children as they played at the park or walked to and from school. The fact that men like this lowlife we had come across were watching, maybe even planning to abuse a child, scared me so much and brought back all those horrendous childhood memories which I tried so hard every day of my life to bury.

Something else was happening too. I had the stomach-churning feeling that my life was being taken out of my control. Up until now, I really had been the master of my own destiny. But now the outside influences, which were pushing me in directions I really did not want to move in, felt very powerful. When I'd taken the decision to become an escort, I could indeed have walked away from that world at any time – my choice and no repercussions – and I did walk away. But now the realisation that the police knew about me, watched me, had opinions about me – it scared the life out of me. I was in too deep. Yet this wasn't a situation I felt I could just walk away from and return to being a legal secretary in the City. All the while I had merely worked as an escort I had that option. Now I had responsibilities towards the girls who worked for me and it wasn't as easy to simply stop.

Chapter Eleven

*K*irsty was no longer able to continue taking the bookings for me and I was back to answering the phones myself six nights a week, which was completely exhausting. That is, until I had a brainwave. Trish and Paula had both worked for Holly as receptionists, each of them taking bookings twice a week. I had no idea what either of them was doing now for work, if they were still working for Holly or had moved on. It was worth a shot – anything for some sleep! I rang Trish and told her all about Crystal Escorts. Was she by any chance looking for a job? Would she be interested? Did she happen to know if Paula might be interested too? We arranged to meet up for lunch over in Croydon where Trish lived, and Sarah also met us there – she would continue to do the odd night as a sort of relief worker, 'Relief from the old man,' she joked.

We worked out quite a simple system. I continued to make the calls on a Monday morning to work out which night the escorts would be available. By now there were also three girls working for me who didn't drive so I also had drivers to co-ordinate for them. Then I made a call to Trish and Paula – I had a conference call facility put on the phone and the three of us would chat about which nights we could or couldn't work.

Life ticked on by fairly uneventfully for a while. By August the agency stabilised at around 45 to 50 bookings a week. The girls, guys and drivers working for me did their jobs and sent their money in without a hitch, and everything was going well.

There was hardly ever a dispute with the girls over money. Mainly this was because of the type of girl I recruited – no drug addicts, only women with real-life responsibilities, strong enough to cope with the second half of a double life. But also I tried to be as straightforward and direct with the girls as I was with the clients. That way everyone knew where they stood and what the boundaries were.

This also extended to my record-keeping. Though at the outset I felt like an amateur, I always wanted to do it right. As the agency grew, my computer came to my aid and I created an Excel spreadsheet which laid out the evenings each girl was available. Under each girl's name for every booking there was the booking length, client's name, address and landline. Every Monday the escorts sent in their money – in cash – by guaranteed next-day delivery, so it was insured and traceable. On the Tuesday I would bank the cash and pay for the next week's advertising. As each girl's money arrived, I would check it against the spreadsheet and tick it off. The girls knew the system – most of them had visited the office at one time or another and seen it in action. And, I suppose, when you are also their agony aunt and confidante, the relationship is less likely to be abused.

Around this time Sharon and I took her youngest and my four younger kids to Center Parcs in Belgium and had a fantastic time. We had become good friends and relaxed easily with each other. I think this was probably because we trusted each other so much and the value we each placed on our friendship was priceless. We knew everything about each other, looked after each other's kids and secrets, aspirations and dreams. The industry we were a part of mainly consisted of fabrication and façade, but Sharon and I had a friendship based on the understanding of one another's experiences, the agony of debt, failed relationships and the burning desire to be happy and secure. During our holiday the agency didn't collapse without me, and September came around all too soon.

With the new term starting and, thanks to Trish and Paula doing a little more time in the evenings, I was able to make myself more useful around the school. David and I had attended the previous term's Summer Ball and had a great time. Debbie, my best friend at the school, was just kissing her little boy, Chip, goodbye and I watched as he and Victoria linked arms and went into school together. How far away from my other world this all seemed. Debbie looked round and, spotting me on my own, waved to me in the playground.

'Got time for a coffee?' she said. 'I think we need a chat.' Debbie knew that I ran an agency and thought it was just fine; she certainly never passed any comment to the contrary and kept the information to herself. I would've hated the other mothers to have hold of such a juicy piece of gossip because there was a clique of mothers who fell into the somewhat self-righteous category. They all had seemingly perfect marriages, went to church on a Sunday, attended every function possible at school, and were all-round pillars of the community.

I followed Debbie back to her house and she made us some breakfast.

'Look, Dawn,' she said, as she sat down at the table and proceeded to butter some toast. 'A few of the God-squad crowd have been asking questions about you. You know, what you do for money. Five kids at the school – it doesn't take a genius to work out how much that comes to each year. And your kids are never dressed out of the second-hand shop, are they?'

I took her point. Didn't they have anything better to do than gossip about me? She reckoned I should just drop a few hints about how much money I'd come away with from my divorce, and how well-off David was.

'Thanks, I'll bear it in mind,' I said.

Anyway, Debbie would listen out for any more unsavoury gossip and let me know. This bunch of women thought they were something really special. Why couldn't they just mind their own business? I could just imagine how much delight these women would take from the discovery that a mummy from school ran an escort agency. It would be the talk of the school gate for weeks. I could just hear the clicking of tongues and the comments. I wondered how they would feel if they ever found out that a couple of the daddies from school were regular users of that same escort agency and, even more scandalous, one of those daddies was the husband of one of their own. Of course, I had no intention of ever letting that slip out because of the damage it would cause, and I wasn't out to destroy anyone's marriage.

We had the school revue in a couple of weeks' time, a sort of talent show, the highlight being the sketch that the mothers from the PTA put on. This year we were doing a spoof of Riverdance. It was absolutely hilarious, all of us with matching outfits, short kilts and flowing capes but each with different footwear. I hadn't decided what to wear yet, but now I knew! Debbie wore carpet slippers, someone else wore green wellies, Kerry wore pink fluffy mules and me, well, I borrowed Christina's thigh-high black leather boots complete with six-inch heels. How I managed to walk in them, let alone dance is beyond me but I did and boy, did I get some laughs and dodgy glances from certain people!

Debbie circulated a few comments about how rich David was and it seemed to work for a while at least. Speculation died down and some other poor woman became the brunt of the current week's gossip. Now that Debbie had brought this to my attention I was constantly on guard and maybe I was just being paranoid, but I now felt really uncomfortable as I waited for the kids to come out of school. I had often waited with Debbie, standing at the school gate on the edge of the car park, chatting to other mums and dads as we waited for our offspring to emerge from their classrooms. Now I felt almost embarrassed, preferring either to wait in my car or sit with Debbie in hers. Debbie said I was being silly and should ignore these women, but their sidelong looks and their whispered conversations really did hurt.

I was standing in the queue at the bank when the 'Dam Busters' theme tune blared out of my handbag. Finally fishing out my mobile, much to the relief of everyone else in the queue, I answered.

'Hi Dawn, it's Ray, can you talk?'

Ray? Ray? Oh no, Policeman Ray! 'No, I can't actually. Can you give me 20 minutes?' He did so, and this time when he called I was on my way home – yes, all hands-free and legal: who knows, he could have been following me! In any event, it certainly wasn't what I expected.

'Just thought you would like to know, your client is now behind bars and will be for a bloody long time if I have anything to do with it. We found so much stuff . . . well I won't go into it but I want to say thank you, that's all. And sorry about Tony; I think he came in on the attack – but you're not like the other tarts we deal with. Sorry, not that you are a tart . . . I'll shut up now, shall I? Look, you weren't what he expected and you don't have a history. Okay? Thanks, and please, call me if there is ever anything else.'

I said I knew what he meant and no offence taken. I felt like a million dollars – as if everything I had done, everything about being a prostitute then running the agency was worthwhile because it had led to one less monster on the streets. I rang Isobel, who was ecstatic.

Chapter Twelve

With the school term now well underway, and in spite of some hitches with my eldest, Emily, who was just being a normal teenager, acting up, my attention was back onto Victoria again. We'd been given a date for the operation, which would determine if her heart was damaged. Far from being scared by all these visits to the hospital and the constant monitoring, she still thought it was all one big adventure. After the last check-up we'd gone to Harrods and had ice creams on the ground floor, before trailing up to the toy department and letting Victoria choose a present, not only for herself but for her brothers and sisters too.

The following week, Victoria and I arrived at the Royal Brompton, found the children's ward and she settled in, so well in fact that she immediately found someone to play with and completely forgot about the reason she was there. After the preliminary checks, blood pressure, a urine sample, an ECG and numbing cream on the backs of her hands for the IV drips, my little girl was taken away to ascertain exactly where the missing beats were occurring within her heart. Sarah, who was Victoria's godmother, had bought her a gorgeous fluffy pink pig, which Victoria named Muddy. Muddy was waiting for Victoria when she came round and still sits on her bed today. Now all we had to do was wait for the results.

Victoria recovered beautifully and two days later we went home. Debbie's son, Chip, came to see her at home and had brought with him a card made and signed by all the children in her class. Victoria was desperate to get back to school to tell all her friends about her exciting adventure and to get back to her rugby and hockey.

The following Monday, resisting the urge to phone the hospital to see if Victoria's results were in yet, I phoned all the girls to see how their weekend had gone. The only person I hadn't been able to contact was Lucy. I tried her at her day job too, but one of her colleagues said she'd taken a week's holiday at the very last minute because her husband had come home unexpectedly.

In one way that put my mind at rest, at least it accounted for Lucy not picking up the phone, but now I was concerned for her: why had her husband come home? Had he found her out? Maybe he'd discovered where the money was coming from, and it definitely wasn't from doing overtime at work! I tried Lucy's number again later in the evening and this time she answered the phone. As soon as she heard my voice she responded in a whisper, 'I can't talk, he's here.'

'Lucy, is everything okay? You weren't expecting him, were you? Please give me a call as soon as you can . . . one last thing, does he know?' I asked her.

'No, it's okay, I'll speak to you next week when I come back to work,' she told me, and I breathed a huge sigh of relief.

The next day passed quickly as I dealt with all the usual stuff that working mothers have to deal with, from the logistics of the kids' activities to filing my receipts for the accountant. Trish was answering the phones that evening so I switched off. I started thinking about Lucy again – surely she must have had a moment to use the phone? She'd said her husband didn't know about the agency and that she was okay . . . but it didn't stack up. I had a growing feeling that she was trying to avoid me as her agency commission fees hadn't arrived that morning. There had to be a reason for it, she was always so organised and reliable.

Then I had an idea. I asked Paul, a driver for the agency, to drive to Lucy's house on his way to pick up his lady for the evening just to see if everything looked okay. Paul phoned me to say that just after he'd pulled into Lucy's cul-de-sac, her husband had come out of the house, climbed into his car and driven off. I took advantage of my luck, dialled Lucy's number and she picked up straight away.

'I can't talk, he's here,' she whispered, her voice sounding terrified.

'Oh Lucy,' I said, 'don't be silly, I know he's not.'

At which point she burst into tears and then, after I made some consoling noises, she told me a client had bounced a cheque on her, and she'd spent all she'd earned the previous week and didn't have any money to send me.

'Lucy, do you have any idea how worried I've been about you? Why on earth didn't you just tell me? Believe it or not, sometimes this sort of thing happens and we can find a way around, but just to ignore me is totally ridiculous. Have a think about it, then ring me in the morning and let me know when you next want to work. I know your husband is around at the moment so obviously leave it this week till he's gone again. Let me have the details of the client who bounced the cheques and I'll see what I can do. They don't like even carefully worded messages asking for payment being left on their answerphones.' One more reason for insisting on a listed landline number from our clients.

Lucy mumbled about how sorry she was and how she'd never try to hide from me again, however difficult the situation might be. She seemed so relieved to hear that I wasn't angry with her. What I found concerning was that she didn't feel she could ring me about the problem. The general rule, of course, was no fee, no more jobs – all the girls knew it had to work that way. But I'd always tried so hard to be as different as I could from the other sort of people that run agencies – never threatening or demanding, always trying to put myself in their shoes. And, in reality I had no real power, or influence, did I?

When I thought about it, first it was the police, and now Lucy was, making assumptions about the sort of person I was. I began to see that no matter how much you try to separate yourself from the rest of the pack, people will fall back on stereotypes.

Chapter Thirteen

*J*ust a few days after Victoria had undergone her operation, a letter arrived inviting us back to see Dr Astley to discuss the findings. I dreaded the arrival of each and every one of these letters, as I was so convinced the news would be bad.

We sat once again in Dr Astley's office whilst Victoria, oblivious to the trauma going on in my head and my heart, played with a magnetic farmyard scene. Dr Astley smiled at her before turning her attention to me and Paul.

'Victoria has a condition called supraventricular tachycardia. Her heart misses beats and sometimes, for no apparent reason, beats too fast. She may well grow out of it but she might not. The problem is that the damage is too close to the wall of her heart so for now, the best thing is for her to take the beta blockers and wait.'

I could see Paul was hurting too but, as usual, he was hiding his feelings. Obviously it wouldn't have helped to cry in the doctor's office, especially in front of Victoria, but Paul seemed unable to convey his worries, only asking the occasional question. Even when we were alone and Victoria was being weighed and measured by the nurse, he just stared ahead and wouldn't talk to me. I cried then, when Victoria couldn't see me and Paul, for all the hurt he was feeling, couldn't comfort me or even tell me that he was hurting too.

The doctor also said that, although they could try to fix the damage so that Victoria didn't have to take tablets indefinitely, because of her heart murmur the risk involved in the operation was too great, especially when the success of the operation couldn't be guaranteed. So, there was no choice at all. Victoria would continue to have regular check-ups and take her tablets. I would worry forever and try not to wrap her in cotton wool.

Victoria had previously seen a dietician at the hospital and we had another appointment with her now. She went over the advice she had given us before.

'You must be clear then, about the things she has to avoid. No caffeine, which means no Coke, chocolate, coffee or tea – unless of course it's decaffeinated. No glucose drinks and none of those dextrose energy drinks either.' She handed me the checklist. Just more things to remember, but things that could be the difference between life and death.

To this day Victoria hasn't had any chocolate or a can of Coke and I try to feed all the kids as healthily as possible. Victoria has a very healthy appetite and is used to eating carrots and yogurt, and she often has carob- and yogurt-coated raisins from the health-food shop. She never bats an eyelid if the other kids have chocolate, which makes it all the easier to bear. The most wonderful thing about my little girl is that she is able to carry on as normal – which is great, considering she is sports mad. But in spite of all the reassurances, there are times when I wonder what her future holds. Victoria knows she has health problems and takes them all in her stride, dealing with them as if they were nothing. Whenever I feel afraid, I only need to think of her.

Chapter Fourteen

S haron was sitting at my table with a half-empty mug of coffee, whilst telling me how, that very morning, she'd received the most amazing bouquet of flowers. Normally she'd have loved the fact that someone had done this for her, but they were from her regular client, Colin, and this meant that he knew where she lived. How on earth had he found out where she lived? How many times had I told the girls, over and over, that they must never, ever, give their home addresses to anyone they visited?

Colin had taken to seeing Sharon at least three times a week and, after a while, she hadn't complained. After her blitz on the house, he'd started keeping it clean and tidy. For his part, he couldn't quite believe his luck. Here she was, this lovely lady, coming to see him whenever he wanted and staying for as long as he liked. Of course, he gave her money, but he saw that, I suspect, as a present rather than what it really was – a fee for services rendered. I always felt, reading between the lines, that Colin saw himself as a type of father figure to Sharon. It was as if he felt happy to have someone who needed him at last, even if it was for financial reasons. He'd taken to writing her love letters, which he'd give to her when she visited, as well as all the little presents. He'd even said one evening that he wished he could buy her an engagement ring. Sharon tried not to take any of this seriously but it was clear that Colin was in love with her, and the situation was getting out of control.

Sharon had told me once before that Colin had offered to pay the odd bill for her whenever she mentioned how short of cash she was. What she hadn't told me was that she had been accepting his money. Taking the agreed amount for a service provided is one thing, but allowing the relationship to develop into something else is what I always warned the girls against. Sharon admitted that Colin had paid a few instalments on her car and her council tax bill. I couldn't believe how greedy she had been, but now the regret was all over her face.

As we sat in my kitchen, we pondered how Colin could have found out where she lived. He could have followed her home one night, but that also meant he would have followed her from his house to her next booking and sat around for hours until she finally drove home. Or perhaps he had hired a private detective. Whatever or however, Sharon's simultaneous lives had been interfered with and were now in serious danger of colliding. There wasn't much I could do other than advise her not to see him again. I offered to speak to Colin and to tell him that he must not bother her at home. But Sharon was scared. What if he wouldn't take no for an answer? She was torturing herself and I didn't know how to help her.

I didn't have an immediate solution, but I did know how it felt to have one's normal life suddenly threatened like this. Back at the very beginning of my working career as an escort, I visited a client in a hotel room in Bexleyheath. He eventually became a regular of mine, calling about once a fortnight. Everything was fine for six months or so. I knew very little about this man, who told me his name was Chris, other than he was an accountant, aged about 50, married with two kids and lived up in Norfolk somewhere. I had turned up at the hotel he always stayed at, at the usual time – it was always about 9.00 pm for an hour. He sometimes gave me an extra £20, nice but not earth-shattering. There had been a few little presents, like a couple of CDs and once a teddy bear, but that was it.

One night he opened his wallet and said that as he didn't have an awful lot of cash, would I mind taking a cheque. He gave me £100 in cash and wrote a cheque for £60. Chris asked me who he should make the cheque payable to and, sticking to my rules, I said to leave it blank and I'd fill it in later, which I did. The hour passed by and I left with my cash and cheque, driving on to the next job.

A couple of weeks later Holly phoned whilst I was picking the kids up from school. She told me Chris had phoned and could I be at the hotel in Bexleyheath, at 9.30 pm this time. It was about a half-hour drive so I could leave home slightly later that night, which was great. I arrived at the hotel and went straight up to the room. By now I was quite used to the layout of the place and if you walk into a lobby confidently no one ever questions whether or not you're a guest. I knocked on the door and Chris opened it with only a bath towel wrapped around him, as was his custom. At least I knew he was showered and clean, which was more than some clients managed.

I remember how he shut the door behind me and said, 'Good evening, *Dawn*.' How the hell did he know my real name? I was horrified and could feel the blood draining from my face. He must have known the impact this would have on me, but I think even he was shocked at how stunned I was. I plonked down on the bed, dropping my bag by my side. Why . . . ? How . . . ? Oh yes, I knew exactly how Sharon was feeling. The difference was that Chris just did it to be clever, because he could. He had called his bank manager saying that he'd forgotten to fill in a cheque stub, so could he please have the cheque sent to him so he could reconcile his accounts. And there, large as life, was my name. A few checks – electoral roll, directory enquiries – and he had an address as well as a name. I have an unusual surname, there aren't many of us about, so it wasn't that hard to track me down. Then a credit check, as he knew when my birthday was (after some carefully worded questions about my star sign) and, hey presto, loads of information. Thankfully Chris never used any of this information to make my life difficult, but he so easily could have.

As we chatted, Sharon finally told me the full story. It wasn't just the odd few pounds extra that he'd given her. It was thousands.

In addition to the car payments and council tax, he had paid off a credit card bill and a couple of store cards, which alone amounted to several thousand pounds. She hadn't asked him for the money, but Colin had been constantly bemoaning the fact that she worked at all – he insisted that he wanted to take care of her and that he could easily pay her debts. Sharon had hesitated at first, wondering how on earth he could possibly afford to do this. In an attempt to prove how trusting he was, he'd shown Sharon his bank statements – he was loaded. So, in a moment of weakness, she let him write cheques totalling £4,800.

Sharon was by no means debt-free but the money had made a huge impact on her monthly outgoings. It was now obvious how he'd found out her address. After all, he'd seen the various statements and bills, all addressed to her at home. Sharon knew that the whole situation was self-inflicted and, after a few comments about her stupidity – more because I felt I should rather than because it could help – we tried to think of a way out of the problem.

I was taking the bookings that evening and, as I suspected, Colin phoned. When he asked for Sharon I said she'd not yet confirmed she was available, but I'd call her and get back to him. I rang Sharon with the news.

'He called just now. I said I'd call you to see if you were available. What do you want to do?'

'This can't go on,' she announced. 'I'll go round now and put things straight.' Her tone was so forthright, but I sensed she was still convincing herself. Then she piped up, 'But what if he gets angry, demands it all back? What if – ?'

I cut her short, 'You could say you're still hurt from your last relationship. You're not ready for another one . . . it would be unfair on him . . . you know.'

'But that won't be the end of it, I know it. He's obsessed. He knows where I live and everything.'

She was right. We'd have to be more devious. She'd have to disappear on him.

'Okay, love, here's a plan: your house is up for sale, so why not just keep him happy till it goes through? He won't know where you've moved to. Change your mobile number and when he calls us I'll tell him you just left the agency and I don't know where you've gone.'

We agreed this was at least a start. Sharon knew that she was at the very least partly responsible for this situation and, whilst I understood how difficult it was to turn down a way out of the financial mess she was in, it was clear to us both she had taken things too far.

'Go on, it'll be a laugh . . . come, oh go on,' Debbie went on and on. The PTA was running a murder mystery quiz night and Debbie was trying her hardest to persuade me that I would really enjoy it. It was a sort of Cluedo thing, in aid of school funds, so I eventually said yes, put the date in the diary and rang David at work to see if he fancied it. He said yes so I bought two tickets. There were eight people to a table, and it was held in the school hall, with everyone bringing their own drinks and nibbles. A whodunnit-type play was performed on the school stage and then we had a break. It was actually quite an amusing evening, trying to work out whodunnit, with what and in which room. I had the additional challenge of figuring out where I'd seen one of the actresses before – in fact she was a neighbour of David's. I don't know who was more surprised – her or us. As we sat and chatted to the other people on our table I became aware of a few nods in my direction, glaring looks and little asides. I asked Debbie what was going on and she said to take no notice as the rumours had started again. Take no notice, she said, a few stupid rumours, that's all.

One of the mothers asked me what exactly it was that I did. She'd really put me on the spot so I just said I ran an agency, but she persisted. A sort of introductions agency, I replied, before excusing myself and catching up with my darling daughter Deborah, who'd appeared just in the nick of time.

I sat in Debbie's kitchen the following morning and moaned about the clique of mothers. Debbie said she'd been meaning to tell me about all the gossip and speculation but we had both been busy, what with the kids and work and everything else.

'Don't worry about it, they'll pick on someone else next week,' she assured me.

Marie, in the meantime, was turning out to be a magnet for the strangest scenarios, but, as she often reminded me, being a nurse in the Accident and Emergency department of a busy hospital, there wasn't much she hadn't seen in her time. However, one booking required her to put all her skills to use. Looking back on it, the evening in question was straight out of a comedy sketch, but at the time it was far from funny. Marie had gone to see Bill, a regular of hers who was a widower, aged about 65. Bill was pleasant enough, didn't need much to keep him happy and they always sat for a while afterwards whilst Marie made them a cup of tea and chatted about his grandchildren, this, that and the other. On this occasion, Marie had come back from the kitchen carrying two cups of tea on a tray with some biscuits, still wearing only her skimpy underwear, just as Bill liked. She thought for a fleeting moment that he'd dropped off to sleep in the chair after his exertions, but to her horror, she quickly realised that he was either unconscious or – a horrible thought – dead. Being a nurse, she obviously knew what she had to do, but this situation also called for a little improvisation.

She called 999 and calmly informed the voice on the end of the phone that she was visiting a friend and thought he'd suffered a heart attack. After she had done all she could for him, Marie nipped out to her car and grabbed the tracksuit and trainers she kept in the boot. Making a quick change and wiping off her red lipstick, Marie was dreading the questions she'd get asked and was thinking of possible answers. 'Oh, he was my friend's dad and I sometimes looked in on him,' she told Rob from the ambulance, whom she knew from work. With Rob and his partner focused on their work, Marie gestured to the police officers, who had now arrived and took them aside. 'Look, I have to tell you the truth. I'm an escort, I work for Crystal Escorts.'

Marie went over the events of the last hour or so, much to the amusement of the young coppers, one of whom couldn't help grinning. What a way to go, they all agreed. Marie was just anxious to get away. The ambulance left with Bill, and Marie asked the police what would happen now. Obviously they were in a dilemma, so they took her details, her car registration, checked her ID and told her they would be in touch.

About half an hour later I received a phone call from my friendly policeman, Ray, by which time Marie and I were sitting in the office, toasting Bill with a nice drop of brandy. Marie was certainly relieved she took her payment upfront, as she couldn't see herself searching through a dead man's pockets! True to his word, Ray was trying to help.

'Hello again, I think you know why I'm ringing. What the hell are we going to tell his kids? Your old man died with a smile on his face?'

Ray went through the formalities and I confirmed that I'd taken a booking for Marie to see Bill that evening as I had done on many other evenings. Ray was quite satisfied that everything was above board. Sad as it was, the evening's events had given everyone a chuckle. In the end we agreed it would be best just to say a neighbour had noticed the back door was open and had gone in to investigate. Bill was a lovely man, lonely for a bit of female company, and none of us could see any reason to shatter any illusions his family might have had. As far as we were all concerned, Bill deserved to take his secret with him, God rest his naughty soul!

The following day was Saturday, and the whole family wrapped up warm, ready for a walk by the river with Scooby. After a lovely afternoon at Upnor, we came home and I began to think about dinner. Just as I was starting on a casserole, the phone rang. It was Marie. 'Dawn, I think I'm being followed, can I come over? I don't know what to do.' The past came back to haunt me, a lifetime away before David knew where I was going every night, when he had no idea how I was making my money and didn't believe a word I told him. Private detectives – I was honoured by two sets at the same time – had been following me, as Paul's mother had had the same suspicions. Marie was beside herself with worry so I tried to placate her and told her to come right over. David grinned, said, 'Spooky – déjà vu or what?', and kept the kids amused whilst Marie and I reviewed the facts.

Marie was scared. 'I keep seeing the same car everywhere for the past few nights I've worked. It isn't my imagination, I know it's happening. At first I put it down to the Bill thing, and then tiredness, you know . . . But I wrote the registration down and I've seen the car everywhere I go.' Although Marie wasn't married and didn't have a boyfriend, she lived in constant fear of being found out – after all, she had her grown-up sons to think about, and her parents were still alive too. She'd had a close shave when she had to let the ambulance drivers in to attend to Bill, but she was pretty sure she'd got away with her secret safe from her colleague. Who on earth could be following her? She just couldn't work it out. I said she should take a break if that was what she wanted. I told her about David and my ex-mother-in-law but she said she couldn't see her ex, or anyone else for that matter, being interested. Obviously I was worried that it was a client and she might be going through the same scenario Sharon had.

I called Marie on Monday morning as per usual and she told me the nights she would be working for the week. She wanted to work that night and, yes, she was feeling up to it. It was Paula's night on the phones so I mentioned that Marie might have a problem and put her in the picture. None of us had long to wait because at 8.30 that night all hell broke loose.

Marie had a 9.00 pm booking and was just about to drive off when another car pulled into her driveway. Out jumped her youngest son, Darren, and he started tearing into her. He was screaming and shouting, calling Marie every obscenity in the book. Marie was screaming back at him – it was her life and she could bloody well do what she wanted. Darren started to cry, how could she, how could she be so disgusting? It was revolting, de-grading, sick. He would tell his brothers and they would stop her. No mother of his was going to be a prostitute. Marie tried to get into her car but Darren pulled her back, hurling even more abuse. By this time one of the neighbours, a burly chap, appeared and restrained Darren long enough for Marie to get inside her car and drive over to me.

None of her sons lived at home with her. So when Marie had told them that she was doing extra shifts with a nursing agency to save for a place in Spain, they had no reason to disbelieve her. It was only when Darren was making his way home after a night out and noticed his mum's car parked outside a house in Maid-stone at 3.00 am that her story began to unravel. As far as he knew, she was at work that night. So, when he spoke to Marie the following evening, he asked her if she'd worked the previous night and how the agency nursing was going, Marie did what all the escorts had become so used to doing – she lied. She told her son that, yes, she'd been at work and, though it was tiring, the money was good, so she'd continue to work for the nursing agency for the foreseeable future.

Darren was puzzled: why would she lie? It was definitely her car but it was parked miles from the hospital where she claimed to have been. At first he thought she must have met someone but was too shy to talk about it. Marie, however, sealed her own fate by leaving a building society passbook on the kitchen table one day. Darren had popped home to pick up a jacket he's left there, and, seeing the book on the table, wondered how far his mum had got towards the deposit for the Spanish villa – a goal he secretly felt was impossible. He nearly choked when he saw her account balance and then looked at the regular deposits over the last nine months. Darren was stunned at the money Marie had stashed away. So he followed her for a couple of nights and worked it out for himself.

Marie's experience was the result of a calculated risk. She knew from the start, just as I had, that her new part-time job was definitely not something her family and friends would find acceptable. Marie had played Russian roulette and had just lost. The shot had been fired and now she needed a few days to pass to let Darren cool off before she launched her damage-limitation exercise.

Darren told his two brothers about their mother's activities as he had threatened to. They were obviously shocked and stunned, but sometimes support comes from the unlikeliest quarters. Marie's daughter-in-law Katie, herself a mother of two, persuaded the brothers that they had no right to judge the woman who had literally slaved all her life to give them the best she could. Even the dream house in Spain was intended as a family place. The brothers were suitably chastised by this voice of reason, which was quite a turn-up for the books, because before that moment, Marie had always assumed Katie disliked her.

Chapter Fifteen

Why did I let Debbie talk me into these things? Why didn't I just send in a bottle of wine for a raffle prize like any other sane mother would do? Tomorrow was Saturday and it was the Christmas Fayre at school. I had been cajoled into making some of my famous fairy cakes for the cake stall. The problem was I had to make rather a lot of them because the number of volunteer bakers had dwindled to two or three. That was all I needed on a Friday night off! I moaned about it but didn't really mind; it was for school and for the benefit of my kids as well as all the others. It would have been useful to have had a few other mums baking too, but it was always the same few who did the bulk of the helping out at these functions. Actually I think that's true of any school PTA but I did have the help of Loretta, another mum from school, which made things a little easier.

Trish was taking the bookings that night so I popped into the office at about 6.00 pm and tapped the code into the phone to divert it to her. Usually it responded with two beeps and then a long continuous tone, but on this occasion it didn't. I rang the phone company, who apologised – until a fault was fixed there was no divert facility available. In the meantime, I was going to have to manage both the phone and the cakes.

Loretta was fully aware of what I did; actually, it now seemed to be common knowledge. After being asked outright at the whodunnit night about what I *really* did, the news had spread like wildfire. Shortly afterwards, a mother had collared me in the playground and told me that it wasn't too late to turn to God because He would save me. Maybe, I thought, but in my experience He doesn't pay the school fees. In fact it was her husband who was making a contribution to my school fees as a regular subscriber to Crystal Escorts' services! Perhaps she should have been having a word a little closer to home.

In many ways, I was relieved the whole thing was out in the open, no longer a secret. I'd had enough of secrets to last a lifetime. So when they asked me exactly what sort of agency it was that I ran, I almost relished being totally honest. I checked up on the legality again just to reassure myself, so that I could clearly explain the situation because the last thing I wanted was anyone causing me problems with the police. Not that they didn't already know about me, of course. It did still bother me that people seemed to have a pretty good idea of what I was doing, but since they did, I felt that it would be unwise to say anything but the truth when I was asked a direct question. The whole playground gossip thing is like Chinese whispers. Once one person gets a sniff of a scandal, then whatever it is gets doubled, trebled . . . and when it eventually does the full circle, the original piece of juicy information has become so badly distorted that it's barely recognisable. So, after talking to Debbie, I just short-circuited the loop by coming right out with the truth.

With just a few moments to go before Loretta arrived, I checked on the kids. The two oldest were sleeping over at friends' houses that night and the younger children were in the lounge, watching a film. David was playing badminton after work with a friend and would not be home for a few hours yet. All was peaceful, for the time being at least. The doorbell rang and I let Loretta in. She wasn't someone I knew that well, but when I'd been volunteered into doing the cakes, Loretta had suggested we could share the job, since Debbie was already doing something else. Loretta admired the kitchen and unloaded her contribution towards the imminent bake-athon. I explained the problem with the phones and how I had to answer it.

'It's okay,' she said straight away. 'I've heard the rumours. I know where to come if I'm ever skint!' She'd made a joke of it all, her way of telling me that she wasn't bothered, wasn't judging, she was here to do her bit for the school and my business was my business. In fact as the evening progressed, we chatted about my 'work stuff' as the subject became unavoidable.

Knowing what kind of person was likely to be on the other end, Loretta seemed to find it quite amusing when I had to run off and answer the phone. Then of course it rang and rang and rang. Great for business, but when you have a bowl of cake mix under your arm and you're in the middle of carefully measuring red food colouring to make six-dozen pink cakes, it's a complete nightmare. The children were packed off to bed at their appointed times with kisses and story tapes because, as much as I strive to be a good mother, bedtime stories just couldn't be accommodated that night. I had agreed to make the six-dozen fairy cakes, some gingerbread men, a coffee sponge, a lemon sponge and a plain Victoria sponge, but it was a slow process because the phone kept ringing. There were the usual enquiries interspersed with the odd booking whilst Loretta baked for Britain. We were inching towards our goal and by 10.00 pm had the fairy cakes and gingerbread men cooling on wire racks. Not much of a result for the time spent, but we were doing our best.

Then Carl rang. Carl lived in a fabulous house, more like a mansion really, out in Newington. He was having one of his legendary impromptu bashes and would like five of my most delightful ladies to join him and his guests. The girls always had a fun night at Carl's parties, quite a contrast to the majority of their bookings. He wanted them there for midnight, 'Usual attire,' he added. Carl was very visual, like a great deal of men, and liked the whole scantily-clad, PVC, thigh-high boots and latex-gloves look. After what felt like a hundred phone calls to co-ordinate the booking, it was agreed that the five girls would meet at my house and travel in convoy.

I have to say that Loretta coped so well with the situation. I'm not sure if she was just completely overwhelmed with the procession of people who were arriving at my house or if it was because she found the whole thing completely fascinating.

As the girls started to arrive I introduced them to Loretta, who was covered in cake mix. I needed to think about where they could change. I looked down at one of the chopping boards, with its insane sprinkling of icing sugar. Which reminded me – first of all I needed to talk to them all about the copious amounts of cocaine that would undoubtedly be flying around this evening. I had strict views on the use of the stuff and, although I acknowledged that it was unfortunately an occupational hazard, it was also to be avoided. Being high was not a recipe for safety or consensual sex. Giving the girls individual pep talks was one way, but if they were all spoken to together hopefully they would think that one of the others might snitch on them, and control themselves.

The last two girls arrived with drivers in tow. Pete and Trevor sat and chatted about their cars, football, etc – I heard snippets of a typical blokey conversation – while the girls pooled resources and changed into their outfits.

I hardly had a moment to think what the kids might make of this scene. They were used to meeting the girls, but always in their civvies. Now their homely kitchen was beginning to look like an Ann Summers photo shoot. The older kids knew the full story anyway. As for the younger ones, they thought Mummy ran a dating agency – I just hoped they had no reason to wander downstairs but I started to concoct a story in my mind about a fancy dress party just in case they did.

My kitchen thankfully was quite large, with a table and six chairs at one end where the guys had plonked themselves. It was covered in an array of cakes, though not as large an array as I'd hoped. And with Pete and Trevor staring at them, there was a real risk of it becoming an even smaller array. Then slowly the girls emerged from the office looking spectacular. Loretta had just retrieved the last lot of cakes from the oven and Lucy, bless her, started to sort out the mess in the overflowing sink. She was wearing full-length latex gloves so she didn't bother with my pink marigolds!

Unfortunately, the sleek fetish variety of gloves don't come with a practical grooved surface and it wasn't long before a tumbler slid straight through her fingers, hastened by a film of washing-up liquid. There was a crash as it hit the floor, a tiny silence, then an eruption of laughter from all corners of the room.

Jenny picked up a tea towel and leant against the work surface, trying not to topple over in the five-inch patent red shoes she could just about walk in. It was 11.15 pm and the girls had about half an hour to kill, and what an industrious half an hour it became! Marie mixed up the icing and, as she spooned just the right amount onto the tops of the cakes, Pete very gently picked up the tiny Christmas angels and Santa Clauses made from icing sugar and placed one in the middle of each cake.

You wouldn't want to mess with Pete. Pete is man-mountain and has LOVE and HATE tattooed across his knuckles. As he held a little sugar angel between his battered, chubby fingers, he examined it closely. It was then that we heard his gravelly voice say, with not a trace of irony, 'Oh, look, she's got sparkly wings!' Of course that set the whole room off once again.

Dishes were washed, dried and put away; cakes were iced, decorated and stored in Tupperware boxes; work surfaces were wiped down; and the girls left for their booking. Finally we watched Jenny kick off her ridiculous shoes, muttering, 'Oh, I'll put them on when we get there,' as she pulled the front door gently shut behind her. Click.

There was a moment's silence before Loretta, a huge grin spreading across her face, collapsed into fits of laughter, finally managing to push some words out between gasps for air.

'Oh my God! This is the weirdest night I have ever had in my life!'

An hour or so later she headed off into the night, leaving my house and peace descended at last. Oh well, I thought, the PTA may not approve of the agency but they'd certainly approve of our co-operation in the kitchen. Whatever they thought of us, all the girls were parents, or grandparents, as were the two drivers, and really that's all we were, no matter what we did for a living.

Chapter Sixteen

*L*oretta arrived the next morning to help load the cakes into our cars.

'Everything go okay last night?' she asked politely, with a mock-innocent smile.

'Yes, I think a good time was had by all,' I said, returning a grin.

We couldn't stop the giggles as we drove up to school and tried to control ourselves as we approached the driveway. With our precious cargo aboard we took the speed bumps comically slowly and parked as close to the hall as we could. It was one of those gloriously sunny winter days and hopefully there would be a really good turn-out for the Christmas Fayre. We began to unload the cakes, carrying tray after tray into the wide open doors of the school hall.

One of the clique of mothers, stood by directing operations. 'My goodness me, you two have been jolly busy,' she said as we brought in the last of the cakes and laid them all out on the trestle tables we'd been allocated. I could almost imagine one of the gingerbread men winking at me as Loretta suppressed a secretive smile.

'Did you make them all by yourselves or did you have some help?'

Biting my, lip I smiled sweetly. 'Well, a few friends did pop in, so I guess it was a joint effort. Actually, they really got into it and we had a great time. It really made the evening.' Loretta's eyes were watering with the effort of suppressing ther laughter, which only erupted once we were back in the car park.

I still didn't know at this point exactly what Sharon was up to. She had assured me that everything was completely under control with Colin and there were no more problems. When she'd told me of her plans to sell her house and move abroad, I thought it would do her and the kids the world of good. Sharon said she'd made huge inroads into her debts and when she finally completed on the house, she'd finish up the last few debts and start over in a warm country with no worries. I was really pleased for her.

Two nights later, though, Sharon was sitting in my kitchen with her world falling down around her. She had more to tell me about Colin. Things were even worse now, as she'd discovered he'd remortgaged his house to help her buy a place for them both to live. Sharon cried – for herself, her kids, the mess with Colin and for what her life had become.

'You could always go ahead with the sale of your house, tell him you've changed your mind about him and give him his money back,' was about the best I could do. But she said there was absolutely no way he would have that – she had no alternative but to disappear, then she would send him a cheque, otherwise she would never be rid of him. I couldn't believe he had actually remortgaged his house for her.

Ultimately, it was Sharon I really felt for. All she'd ever wanted to do was to support her family, provide for them and protect them. By entering this world she had encountered situations that were so artificial and unusual that you need extra strength, extra strategies to cope with them. This was the real problem; we were all just very normal people attempting to do the best for our families, and this world was not one that we felt at home in. Sharon's motives had only ever been good but her judgement had been clouded by temptation, and now only she could put that right.

A couple of days later I stood at the kitchen sink, planning life in general, when the phone rang. Quickly wiping my hands on a tea towel I grabbed the phone. It was my mother, calling from her home in Germany. The shock in my voice must have been audible because she hesitated and asked if I was still there. After the sports day at school I hadn't heard anything at all from her and now here she was calling out of the blue, chatting to me as if this was an everyday occurrence. Did she really have no idea that this was a massive emotional journey for me, having contact with her again after all these years?

She asked after the kids and said that she and her husband were coming over in a few days, staying with my grandmother, and they'd like to come to see the children. I suddenly felt hurt. Why did she say come and see *the children*? Why not include me and say could they come and see *us all*? Or was I being over-analytical? Why did I crave the love and attention of a woman who had cut me out of her life for seven long years? Meeting her again had been a complete coincidence. Pure chance. It wasn't as if she'd sought me out, missed me or wanted to see me. Or maybe all it had ever needed was an excuse: maybe her pride wouldn't allow her to do anything but rely on chance, on a coincidence. Casually, trying not to let my thoughts betray me, I invited them to dinner on the Wednesday of the following week. I wanted to scream at her, 'Why? Why? WHY?' but I didn't; I just asked her if there was anything in particular her husband didn't like to eat. Why did I allow her to intimidate me? I was a grown woman of 35, not a scared child trying to assert myself. Why did it mean so much to me? We said, 'Goodbye, see you next week!' as if she had always been there and never missed the children's birthdays, Christmases, first words, school plays . . . I put the phone down and sat at the kitchen table, tears pouring down my face.

I called David just to hear his voice – comfort and a cuddle down the phone. There really was nothing he could do from work, only tell me that he loved me and would be home in a few hours. 'Is she really worth it?' he said. 'All these tears, revisiting all that resentment and hurt, all that anger every time you think about her?'

That afternoon I collected the children from school and casually announced over dinner that Grandma would be coming to see them along with her husband. I thought about nothing else all week; what should I cook, whether David would manage to be home for seven, would the kids be starving by then – stupid, petty things which made me even more nervous and anxious, as well as cross with myself for allowing her to get me into such a state.

On Wednesday morning I went shopping for dinner. After deciding that roast beef was probably the safest bet I now stood in the butcher's collecting it. Next I went to the greengrocer's, and finally, the supermarket. As I unpacked my shopping and thought about everything I still had to do, I wondered what she had done to deserve all this effort.

In the end the evening turned out to be a huge anticlimax. A nothing. No momentous anything. Dinner was thankfully perfect: crispy potatoes, vegetables cooked but crunchy, succulent melt-in-the-mouth beef, smooth gravy – not a lump in sight. My home-made apple pie was wonderful and I was happy they were sampling my cooking at its best.

Yes, the meal was good, the kids behaved, David was early and we were all pleasant, but maybe that was the problem. The evening just passed as if nothing had ever happened. It was as if there had never been a suicide or a family ripped to shreds, estranged for years. How could we just pass the salt, have another potato? I don't know what it was I was expecting. Maybe I really did think that she was going to hug me and say sorry, but she didn't, not that night and not any other night. I knew I couldn't have a relationship with her because there would never be a resolution or an explanation. She would get up and walk away if I tried to broach any one of the subjects I needed to straighten out in my head.

My mother and her husband came to dinner again. The children weren't keen about it because she was not the sort of grandma they had imagined. And they knew her visits always made me sad, so that was enough for them. I couldn't help it; I didn't mean to be so transparent in front of the kids. I really did want them to form their own opinions about her. I didn't say horrible things, in fact I didn't say anything at all about her visits. The kids could tell I wasn't happy with her around, but we kept in touch nevertheless.

One day the inevitable happened. She disagreed with something I did and told me so, which was fine. I felt that Emily was quite capable of looking after the other kids for two hours whilst I was shopping a mile down the road. I had left beef stew and dumplings bubbling away in the slow cooker for the children's dinner, had arranged for a friend to drop the kids at home after school and would only be gone a short while. It seems completely ridiculous now to think that she was so put out by my saying that the kids were perfectly capable of dishing up their own dinner and being left to their own devices for a couple of hours. I never heard from her again.

My childhood friend, Gillian, was 40 recently and had a big party to celebrate. Her mother, Elsie, hugged me and said how lovely it was to see me. That hug, the warmth of Gillian's family and the love in Elsie's eyes were real, always have been, and I

155

know that there will always be a cup of tea in the pot any time I ever need one. I've come to realise that the feeling of having somewhere to go, someone to turn to who will be there no matter what, will never come from my mother. It's taken a long, long time to adjust to that fact but, between them, the love of my friends makes up for her ten-fold.

Chapter Seventeen

*C*hristmas had come, and gone, thank goodness. We had arranged things slightly differently this year and it had all been more relaxed. All my children had gone to Paul's parents' house on Boxing Day and stayed overnight. They hadn't seen him at all on Christmas Day but, despite this, the kids had a great time. David had gone to see his children early on Christmas morning and had come home at about 2.00 pm. I didn't cook dinner until early evening and so we had a lovely, relaxing, pleasant day.

It was bliss not to have to do the school run for a few weeks. The kids had friends over to play, and in return went off to play with friends. There were a couple of birthday parties that the children had been invited to so we were all pretty occupied. On New Year's Eve David and I went out for dinner, while the kids went to Paul's parents, who were having a party. As David and I watched the fireworks going off over the river, I made wishes for the coming year. Not resolutions at all, just particular wishes for happiness for each of us – I wished that Alexander would pass his 11-plus exam and get a place at the grammar school, and Victoria, just that she be healthy.

New Year's Day was dry and fine. The kids played in the park as David and I walked by the river with Scooby. I thought about the past year and the women who had become such a big part of my life. Over 30 women had worked for Crystal Escorts during the course of the previous year but the impact that Marie, Jenny, Sharon, Christina, Isobel and Lucy all had on my life was permanent. All the women had played a role, and in their own small ways would continue to do so; but now I thought about how the year had passed for these six people, how their lives had changed so significantly since they had each replied to the advertisement. All six women were very special, truly wonderful people.

One thing they shared, which was also true of me, was that in our lives we had all been through hard times. Christina's mother was an alcoholic who had committed suicide; Jenny's father was an alcoholic; Marie was neglected and violently abused, having her first child at 14. I had been sexually abused by my father, as had Lucy. Sharon had never been wanted, had been emotionally neglected and physically abused. Isobel had been so unceremoniously dumped by her ex. Because we had experienced these traumas, did that give us the strength of character to switch off and do what we had done for our families?

When I first started working for Holly's agency it was because I wanted security and stability for my family. Each of us wanted something so badly we were prepared to use any resource we had to achieve our goal. We had all learned the hard way that, in this life, the only person we could truly depend upon was ourselves. Lucy's husband could depend on her, but he would never know it; and I wondered if he had the strength to allow her to depend on him. I hoped she would never need to find out. I was forever on and off with David – I put it down to the fact that I could never really trust or truly open myself up to anyone. Jenny was single, as were Sharon and Marie most of the time. As much as we were all incredibly strong women, we desperately craved the love and security of a relationship, but none of us could ever give 100 per cent, or ever truly allow our defences to relax and believe there was no hidden agenda. We trusted each other, but only because we all bore the scars from another lifetime.

By now Crystal Escorts was one year old, and I felt that warranted some kind of celebration. There was a very swanky bar in Rochester, The Velvet Rooms, which was the place to go. It had recently been seriously refurbished with that amazing lighting that all the beautiful people liked to be seen under. At least, the people who thought they were anyone special by Rochester's standards. There was a function room upstairs with space to dance and eat – not too large, but intimate enough for what I had in mind. So, I called and spoke to the manager. We agreed a date, discussed the menu, the music and all we had to do was turn up. I had invitations printed, let all the girls, boys, drivers and phone operators know the date, time and place and told all the regulars when they called that we would be shut for one night only. It was all a bit strange because there had never been an occasion prior to this when any great number of us had ever congregated – there had never been a reason to.

Unfortunately, the weather was appalling on the night of the party and, although there was a good turn-out, there weren't as many people as I'd hoped. It had been snowing heavily all over the south-east, although by the evening the snow was at the slushy stage and melting fast. Debbie and her husband were there, as were Kirsty and loads of other friends. I think some of the girls stayed away because they felt either embarrassed or were petrified of being recognised. Jodie, who had been working for me for about three months, arrived in a long blonde wig, in the hope that no one would recognise her. Then Ritchie came with a couple of his gorgeous fire-fighting colleagues who knew about his second job and I offered them jobs on the spot. Some of my friends were desperate to know which of the other guests were escorts, but of course I wasn't about to tell them. We rounded the evening off at a local nightclub and had a great time, dancing until 2.00 am.

David had not come to the party, as yet another stupid row meant I hadn't seen him for a couple of weeks. These days, we had such an up-and-down relationship and argued over so many things. David felt so guilty about his kids, that he failed them because he split up with their mum. It was a huge strain on our relationship and, as much as I tried to understand and sympathise, I was more pragmatic about the situation than David, which I think he interpreted as being uncaring. David also did not like the company I kept, the people I knew and mixed with, and the world I now seemed to belong to, which was completely alien to him. A recent row had turned into a complete silence, as I thought him unreasonable and he felt the same about me. We reached a stalemate and the silence just grew.

Normal business resumed the following day and, still shattered from the party, I was manning the phone. It was about 10.00 pm and I was ironing in the office so I could take the calls. Just as I was reaching for a school shirt, the phone rang. It was Taj, a great favourite of mine. Taj owned an Indian restaurant in Gillingham and liked to see a different girl every time. His family lived in London and he often stayed in the basement flat of the restaurant after a particularly late night, or on a night he took a visit from one of the 'Crystal Ladies' as he called them. We chatted about all the usual – his kids, his wife, the business – and finally, he asked if I had any new ladies. As it happened, I didn't, but undeterred, he booked a visit from Jenny. It had been a long time since he'd seen her so he was happy.

Taj was always inviting me over to the restaurant for a meal and did so again tonight. He moaned that he was offended I would not accept his hospitality so I called his bluff and agreed to come over with a couple of the girls the following week. In fact, he was absolutely delighted, though of course he asked me to be the soul of discretion in front of his staff. I phoned the restaurant the following day and booked a table for three on Thursday for 7.30 pm. I'd asked Marie and Sharon to come along with me – it was early enough for them to work afterwards if they wanted to.

Thursday arrived and we all took our own cars so the girls could go off to their respective bookings afterwards. By chance they both had a booking for 11.00 pm, in different directions, but not too far from the restaurant. Marie told me she had rung Sharon and reminded her to bring a toothbrush for after the meal! We couldn't see Taj when we first arrived but as we were ordering drinks he appeared behind the bar. He glanced around the restaurant and did a double take as he recognised first Marie then Sharon. With a big grin on his face he came over to us and shook hands, saying to me, 'Doctor, so good of you and your colleagues to come. You look very lovely this evening, away from the hospital and your white coat.' I think he overdid it slightly – maybe he was a big *Holby City* fan – but the diners on the other tables certainly didn't cotton on that I was a madam with two prostitutes as companions! The food was fantastic. I would thoroughly recommend Taj's restaurant – not that I can ever publicly name it but, well, the thought is there. Taj sat and had a drink with us, and was the perfect host, insisting that the evening was on the house, which was very generous of him and completely unnecessary, but he said he had invited us and we were his guests, so I gave up protesting and gracefully accepted his hospitality.

As I said, Taj was a lovely man but he was in such a sad situation. An arranged marriage had produced six children. Three of the children were at school doing very well, the oldest was a doctor (I think we were supposed to be work colleagues of his son), one was about to qualify as an architect and he had another at university. He was devoted to his kids, absolutely adored them but he and his wife had never fallen in love. Taj and his wife fulfilled the obligations they felt duty-bound to do for the sake of their families. He was a good provider and his wife cooked and cleaned, and was a good mother. There was no way they were ever going to part – it just wasn't the done thing. Taj was lonely, lonely for companionship, affection and occasionally sex. Who is to judge in a situation like this? I for one could not condemn him for it.

My turn to take the bookings came around the following night and Dennis called at about 10.00 pm. I always dreaded a call from Dennis because I had to be so very careful. A couple of months back a very pleasant lady, Lynda, had joined the agency and worked a couple of nights a week. Her motivation was that she couldn't abide her husband so she was putting together a running-away fund. Lynda had been married for eight years, was aged 34, didn't have any children and had had enough of her husband. The only thing that was stopping her was money. She also knew her husband well enough to know that she wouldn't squeeze her share out of him without a long drawn-out fight. She knew how vindictive he could be after watching him fall out with a business partner, which involved him lying in court about the finances and worse still, getting away with it. Lynda worked full-time and, here was the problem, she was married to Dennis.

She told him she was doing a couple of nights a week answering the phone for a taxi firm when in fact she was driving all over Kent in an effort to earn enough money to escape him. Lynda was quite popular and had a fair few regular clients. She worked the same two nights every week, which her regular clients knew, so she tended to have bookings in advance, which was great for her. Dennis liked to see new girls and was always quizzing the girls he did see about other women who worked for me. Jenny had seen him on one occasion and without realising the implications and in fact thinking she was probably doing the business a favour, she told him there was a new girl, Lynda, who had not long started. Dennis called a couple of weeks later and asked to see her. Paula took the call, knew Dennis was a regular and rang Lynda with the booking. Obviously, as soon as Paula gave Lynda the address Lynda screeched down the phone, 'That's my bleedin' husband!'

That incident really was another nail in Dennis's coffin as far as Lynda was concerned. Her total loathing of the man was now completely justified and she also realised where all their money was disappearing to. Another escort was given the booking and Dennis was quite satisfied, but here he was again, asking for Lynda, whose delights he firmly believed he had yet to sample. I told him that Lynda had left, it just hadn't worked out. 'Shame, I never did get to meet her,' he said. Lynda continued to work and save, Dennis continued to see his wife's colleagues, telling them, and me, that he was single and lonely.

Then there was Mike. Mike owned a very successful carpet shop and had been a client right from the very beginning, the second week in fact. His wife seemed prone to fits of temper and he'd often stay the night at the shop rather than going home to face her after some incident or other had set her off. Mike would have me in fits of laughter with stories about how he'd inadvertantly upset her and in retaliation she had cut his clothes up and thrown them out of the window onto the lawn. How he had then tried to make amends with a long weekend in Rome but she tore the tickets up saying that she'd wanted to go to Prague instead. Mike would never leave her because deep down he loved her and they had been together for such a long time. He blamed her temper on her age but I thought she sounded rather spoilt, myself.

Mike was a man of reasonable means, seeing Marie at 5.15 pm every Wednesday and Lucy at 5.30 pm every Saturday. Occasionally he swapped the days around but it was generally this way. He always rang in the early afternoon on the day of his booking to confirm. He also liked to chat because he was another one who was so lonely. Mike had a son who worked for him. Jason made the deliveries twice a week, on a Saturday and a Wednesday, and only when Mike knew that his son was safely on his way did he entertain Lucy or Marie. In fact, the girls would arrive at the shop at the appointed time, park up, watch for the van to depart and then go into the shop.

Lucy had phoned me once at 6.00 pm saying that the van was still there – what should she do? I rang the shop and Mike answered trying not to appear too flustered.

'I can assure you, madam, that your order will be with you very shortly. In fact my deliveryman is just about to leave. Many apologies for the delay but we've had a technical problem with our van.'

I rang Lucy and relayed the phone call and sure enough, a couple of minutes later the van drove off. Mike had been reading the riot act to Jason, who'd been caught by the police at a routine checkpoint dipping for red diesel. Unbeknownst to Mike, his son had a racket going with a cashier at the garage, handing in fake receipts whilst in fact filling the van with knock-off red diesel and pocketing the money. Mike was furious, not least because of the money and the deceit, but more immediately because a lovely young lady was sitting outside waiting for him! Mike liked to sit and talk to the girls, and they both told me that they thought the sex was an act he went through as an afterthought because he had paid for it so he might as well or he would appear sad and lonely, which of course we all knew he was.

Trish and Paula had their favourite clients, just like I did, and when the three of us got together we all came to the same conclusion that, in the vast majority of cases, the men who rang Crystal Escorts were lonely for companionship, affection and really, when it was all stripped bare, just a cuddle. How did so many relationships end up this way? Why did the love turn sour? Is it just the way we are? Why do couples sit at either end of the sofa instead of curling up together? I don't know, and I don't think anybody else really does either. Observing it is one thing, explaining it is quite another.

Chapter Eighteen

My sister, Joanne, and her partner Ian were going to India for a month. Ian had had a terrible motorbike accident and wanted to get away from the cold weather and relax. He had suffered horrendous injuries but was on the mend and was now able to fly, so they'd booked a month in Goa from mid-February to mid-March. Joanne had asked me if Emily and Alice could go with them. The half-term holiday accounted for some of the time they'd be away, so it still meant that Emily would need to take time off school. This was her GCSE year and she would be doing her mocks as soon as she came back. I phoned her headmistress to see what she thought. Luckily she said that very few girls of Emily's age had the chance to experience another culture so different to our own at first hand and she thoroughly endorsed the trip.

I was so relieved to hear her say that. Emily had always worked so hard at school and I really wanted her to have this opportunity.

So, I told Emily that yes, as long as she revised for her exams while she was away, she could go. She was ecstatic at the prospect, and seeing her reaction diluted my concern over the cost. It was just over £1,000 for each of them and David and I argued about this, which was such a shame, because we had only just started to talk civilly to each other again. He thought I was wrong to let them go, especially Alice, who'd been expelled from school a few months before – he felt I was rewarding her bad behaviour. It was a lot of money and it didn't just stop at the cost of the trip: there was the spending money, the cost of the immunisations, clothes, and the malaria tablets cost a fortune. But what a fabulous experience – I was so pleased for them and wanted them to go. Alice's expulsion had certainly shocked me, and her too, I think. She had been disruptive, had been warned many times and finally Alice and another girl had been expelled, albeit reluctantly, by the headmistress. I completely understood. If I'd been the parent of another girl in her class, paying serious fees for her education, I certainly wouldn't appreciate constant disruption from a couple of badly behaved girls.

Alice hated school and so I tried alternatives. Right now she was happy and was behaving herself, working in a friend's hairdressing salon a few hours each day, a few times a week. She got there and back by herself and worked hard. I guess some children thrive in vocational rather than academic environments, and Alice was one of them. I don't think the sightseeing trips were Alice's highest priority – she was probably more interested in the beaches. But because she had improved her attitude since leaving school and was now trying hard, I was prepared to let her go. Obviously her good behaviour had to continue until she went. David and I rowed constantly about the trip and everything else, and then, very childishly, after a silence of a few days, with neither of us prepared to back down, the silence continued into a week, then two . . .

Some time into the silence between us I stood doing the ironing in the kitchen whilst also attempting to help Emily with her French homework. She was practising a passage for her French oral, reading aloud from a photocopied sheet of paper whilst I was followed from the book. The phone rang, and it was Trish – we had a slight problem. I switched the iron off, my other life on, and went into the office.

Apparently Simon Rawlings had called. Simon was a regular client, using the agency about once every three weeks. He was a very pleasant chap over the phone and all the girls seemed to like him. Simon had seen Sharon five or six times and didn't want to see her tonight, which I knew she would be disappointed about had she known, because she really liked him and he also made bookings of several hours which cost him around £350 a time. Trish had told him which girls were available and he had said no to them all for various reasons. As he was such a good, regular client, Trish told him she would check the availability of another couple of girls and get back to him as soon as possible. We certainly didn't want to lose clients like Simon to a rival agency. I flicked through the roster at the girls who were working tonight. 'Have you asked him if he wants to see Julie or Sophie? What about Tina, I know she's not down to work but you could always try her.' Trish had tried Tina – she was at the bingo with her mum. More wholesome, I thought, but probably not as lucrative. In fact Trish had rung round all the girls who weren't working and unfortunately there was not one who wasn't committed in some way, or didn't have jobs booked already.

'You'll have to go, Dawn. We don't want to lose him and you said earlier that David still hasn't broken his silence, so what's the harm?' Trish put the suggestion to me as if it were just a trip to the library – not what it in fact was, me going back to being a prostitute. She was so blasé about it, and I think her attitude caught me off guard, as if it were something I still did every day, when in reality I was about to make a momentous decision.

Trish was right in a cold, hard way. This was business and, no, I didn't want to lose Simon as a client and, yes, David had been a complete idiot and was being horrible to me, and so I went on, justifying my somewhat unjustifiable actions to myself. 'Okay, but tell him I wasn't planning on being available tonight and am only wearing jeans.'

On autopilot I brushed my teeth, changed my underwear, put a clean shirt on, tidied up my hair and make-up, and asked Emily to watch the kids. I grabbed my mobile, car keys and purse and drove to the hotel he was staying at, which was just off the M20. As I walked to the reception I called Trish. She said, 'I told him your name was Abby. And you only work very occasionally, which is why I didn't automatically think of you. Wow, it's just like old times!' she laughed. I wasn't sure that I found it funny, but I wasn't apprehensive at all, partly because I wasn't exactly a novice, but also because I had spoken to Simon many times on the phone and knew that Sharon thought he was gorgeous. A booking with Simon was an absolute delight as far as she was concerned. I told myself that this was purely a business transaction, a way of retaining a good client. All the moral issues coupled with the fact that I was supposed to be with David despite our current differences, I pushed to one side. I walked through the lobby, called the lift, pushed the button for the fourth floor, walked along the corridor and finally tapped gently on the door of room 418; I was a prostitute again.

Simon opened the door and I just walked in. It was as simple as that. 'Abby? Great. Hi, I'm Simon,' and he held his hand out for me to shake. How typically English, so formal, so well brought up. I wanted to laugh out loud, but I just smiled at this very handsome man. All the time I worked for Holly I never felt attracted to any of the men I was paid to have sex with, which I know sounds ridiculous because a great many of them were handsome, good-looking or however you may want to describe them outwardly. Never once did I ever connect with any of them. Oh, one or two may have left an imprint on my memory but not one ever *touched* me. Simon handed me some money and asked if I could stay for a while. Absolutely, I said as I put it in my bag. I apologised for wearing jeans and explained that I hadn't been expecting to be needed tonight, but he just smiled and said it was fine, no problem at all, and thanked me for coming out. I suddenly felt awkward, nervous and unsure, not because of all the demons jumping around in my head but because of the click I had felt with this man as soon as he opened his mouth and said hello. The last time I had felt like this was the first time I ever saw David, and now the electricity charging between Simon and I could have powered the national grid.

We made love and I wasn't acting, for the first time ever with a client. We talked – well, he talked and I listened. He was married with two children whom he idolised. His wife was ten years older than him. He didn't love her, hadn't made love to her for years. They had nothing in common and did nothing as a family. He had actually left her once but came home after a couple of months because he couldn't leave his kids; the guilt was just too much to bear. So he used the agency because he needed what everyone needs – warmth, love and affection. Simon cuddled me, kissed me, fully, naturally, as I would normally never allow, as if this was something we had done a hundred times already.

The voices in my head screamed at me as I drove away from the hotel. How many hundreds of times had I heard the same sad tale? How many times had men told me that they had nothing in common with their wives, that there was no love, no affection, nothing at all? Surely they couldn't all be lying? Was Simon just one of many men who wanted to have his cake and eat it too? Was he just feeding me a sob story because in some perverse way he felt that he needed to justify his actions to me, a prostitute whose services he was paying for? Is that what they all did? My emotions were cut to shreds over the impact that this man had had on me.

I called Trish to let her know all was okay and made my way home. 'Is he as dishy as all the girls say?' I forced a laugh and said goodnight, I'd catch up with her tomorrow. The picture on the mantelpiece in my bedroom caught my eye as I pulled back the bedspread and moved the pillows around. David and I on holiday, and we looked so happy together. And I had just betrayed him by having sex with another man, and I'd liked it and wanted it. The fact that I'd also taken money for this seemed strangely irrelevant to the deception. I tried to reason with myself once again that David need never know. It was a one-off and that he wasn't talking to me anyway. Who was I trying to kid? I went downstairs to the kitchen and made myself a cup of chamomile tea and went back upstairs, losing myself in a book until I fell asleep.

Trish phoned me the following lunchtime and teased me. 'That Simon phoned and thanked me for sending you.' I could hear her husband Jimmy in the background laughing and saying the other girls had better watch out! I just took down all the bookings, the notes on a couple of the clients and added the night's total to the ledger. I wanted to forget all about Simon, everything about last night and concentrate on the massive pile of ironing I was wading through, yet again, as I stomped up the stairs in my never-ending search for coat hangers. 'Why can't I be like Christina and remember to buy things I run out of or need?' I asked myself as I only found about half a dozen in all the wardrobes. I was trying to think about anything or anybody other than Simon, and I was failing miserably. I went back to the ironing and cried. What had I done?

Chapter Nineteen

*A*mid much excitement, hugs and kisses, promises of post-cards and exotic presents, Emily and Alice flew off to Goa on their great adventure. I was so relieved to get a phone call telling me they'd arrived safely, that it was fabulous, boiling hot and perfectly wonderful. The girls had plans to visit a tea plan-tation, go jet-skiing, go to the markets, see the Taj Mahal, visit temples and ancient ruins, have a sari made up; I was really quite envious and added a trip to India on my own imaginary 'to do' list.

Jenny called in, as was often her custom, one Tuesday morning. She looked really tired after an exceptionally late night, getting the kids to get off to school, then dropping her son at the day nursery before she could collapse in a heap and sleep. Jenny had really turned her life around in the past year. She was very careful with her money, saving as much as she could. She had applied to the local council and managed to swap homes and move from the notorious estate she lived on, to a slightly smaller house, still in Gravesend but away from the violence and crime. She had taken the kids on holiday, their first ever, had decorated their bedrooms and bought a few new bits of furniture. Her home was lovely, the kids were doing well and she felt safe for the first time in years.

I made her a coffee and she yawned as she fished around in the biscuit tin. 'I bet you haven't eaten yet, have you?' I said.

Jenny said she'd eaten last night with the kids so I made her some toast and put a jar of strawberry jam in front of her. She ate her toast and said she needed to get home for a good sleep. Jenny's mum was collecting the kids from school and nursery and they were staying at her house tonight. 'Are you sure you're not overdoing it? I can ask one of the other girls to swap with you if you want the night off, you know, to properly catch up on your sleep.' She said it was fine, and could we try not to book her out until about 9.00 pm so she had chance to catch up on some housework too.

I knew that feeling, constantly trying to fit too much into not enough hours. Jenny picked up her bag, coat and car keys.

'Right, home and to bed with you,' I said as I pecked her on the cheek.

'Well, almost,' she said, 'I have to drop this off for Martin first. You know, the last booking I did last night, Martin in Rochester.'

Oh yes, I knew only too well. Everyone knew Martin Brookman. She produced an A5-size jiffy bag with the name 'Josh' handwritten in capitals on the front, along with the address of a pub in Gravesend. The fear I felt must have been more than obvious because Jenny looked confused.

'What? What is it? It's virtually in the next street . . . it won't take me long, it's a five-minute detour. I've done it before – Martin's always here, there and everywhere, always so busy and his phone never stops ringing – I just help him out now and again. And I've never told him exactly where I live but he knows it's up Gravesend somewhere. It just saves him a journey, and he gives me 50 quid for doing it.'

I picked the envelope up from the table, not quite believing what I was hearing. 'Jenny, what about the rules? You know you shouldn't be doing this. How many times have I told you never to pick anything up or drop anything off for a client?'

'But Dawn, it's Martin and . . . well, I did it because it was him and I felt like I really had to, like he'd be really angry with me if I said no.'

Obviously it was sealed, but I had a good idea what was inside. I had some identical envelopes in the office which I'd bought in bulk at the wholesalers. I told Jenny to sit back down.

'Jenny, have you any idea what's in this envelope, any inkling at all? Surely you've heard about Martin and what he gets up to, the businesses he's involved with, you must know what sort of reputation he has?'

'No, well, I don't know, I thought it might be money, wages or something 'cause I think that's one of the pubs Martin owns. Look, I really never thought about it, he just said it was a message, some business for his manager. I didn't realise all that about Martin. Is he really that bad?'

'Jenny, I'm going to open this and show you – don't worry, I've got another envelope the same – and you'll see it definitely isn't money.'

Jenny looked scared, really petrified, and I could see that it honestly hadn't occurred to her that it was anything except money. Jenny thought she was merely doing a favour for a client who paid her well and saw her regularly.

Martin had intimidated Jenny with his reputation as a hard man, someone who was used to getting his own way. So many unpleasant stories circulated about Martin and his so-called business dealings that it was impossible to separate the fact from the fiction. The stories were often very unpleasant, involved money in great quantities, occasional violence and, all too frequently, drugs. He was not quite at the top of the food chain but I had a feeling that one of these days he would be, and the stunt he was currently pulling on Jenny was probably the tip of the iceberg.

To me, Martin was a voice on the end of the phone making a booking a couple of times a week. To his kind, using an escort agency was an everyday occurrence because they still clung to the belief that the women who worked for agencies were on the same side as them. He reasoned that 'tarts' could be trusted and were always okay for a quick pick-up or delivery. He made it his business to know what was going on in the area he operated and it wasn't long before newly opened Crystal's received a call. He was always courteous on the phone, very well mannered and I

177

think was trying to cultivate an image which would distance him from the more vicious stories which circulated about him. The fact was that he was a bully who made money from drugs and protection rackets, and I didn't intend to get on the wrong side of him. The problem was that in my previous existence I had never knowingly encountered men like Martin – and now they seemed to be everywhere.

I very carefully peeled back the seal of the envelope. Just as I thought: wraps of powder, flattened so as not to feel lumpy or conspicuous. I guessed it was cocaine but wasn't going to take the risk of actually opening one of the wraps. Jenny looked at me with tears streaming down her face, sobbing.

'Oh, Dawn, I've dropped off loads of 'em . . . Christ, oh Christ.'

I put the packages into a new envelope and wrote the name and address on the front, copying the handwriting as best I could. I sealed it and gave the envelope back to Jenny, who was still weeping.

'Look, you're going to have to go through with this now, I'm sorry but you have to. If this doesn't reach its destination you'll be in some serious trouble. I can hardly believe you've been so stupid – but there's no point in beating yourself up over it. You weren't to know, but now you do, so I'll try my best to make sure that you are never put in this position again. Okay? What time did you tell Martin you would drop this off?'

'I said I had to sort the kids then come here, so I'd be at the pub around ten-ish.'

Jenny was fine for time, no problems so far. She just had to get on and do this, and I would make sure this was the last time. How dare he treat one of my girls like that? Martin was well known locally for his exploits on the wrong side of the law; he was also famous for not getting caught. He lived in a fabulous penthouse apartment on an exclusive development overlooking the river. He often saw Jenny, and now I knew why. Jenny was sweet, but so naïve and she just accepted what she was told without question – far too trusting for her own good. I suppose once he realised just how innocent Jenny was, it was a risk he was prepared to take. The thing was, Martin had such a hard-man reputation that no one in their right mind would mess him about.

Jenny pulled herself together, wiped her face and made herself presentable, gulped down a glass of water and promised to ring me the minute the package was delivered and she was out of the pub. I hugged her as she left. Both of us had knotted stomachs by now and were desperate to get the next half hour over and behind us. What on earth was I going to say to Martin next time he rang? Another problem for another day, which I gladly side-stepped. Let's just get this over with first, I thought.

An hour later I was on the phone trying to calm Jenny down after she'd delivered the package. 'Come on, love, just tell me what happened. Get it all off your chest, then we can move on.'

Feeling helpless, like I should be able to instantly make it all better, I listened as Jenny recounted the previous hour. She told me that she'd trembled all the way to Gravesend, but was so glad she knew exactly where she was going and that she knew the area like the back of her hand, having been born and bred there.

Even now, I could hear her at the end of the phone, swallowing her tears as she carried on. She had parked at the back of the pub and felt a pain in her chest from the realisation of how serious this all was, and that today she must look and act just like she did any other day. She had taken a few deep breaths and composed herself. The last thing she needed was to make Josh suspicious. It's amazing what some eye-brightening drops and a bit of make-up could do! She had performed her little heart out. She'd walked into the pub, found Josh, the manager whose name was on the front of the envelope, and even shared a joke with him.

Then she was out, into her car where she burst into tears of relief, of amazement at her own stupidity and trepidation about how we'd handle Martin next time.

'Just go home, and sleep. It's okay, I'll make sure of it, trust me, Jenny, just trust me. It's over.' They were big words, but I was determined to get us all out of this one.

The big silence was still continuing between me and David but I moved it to another compartment to be dealt with some time soon, when I could find the energy and resources. Not tonight though – David could wait. I'd just had Jack read to me and we'd gone through his spellings, then repeated the exercise with Victoria and Deborah. I looked at Alexander's maths homework, digging into the depths of some far-distant memory to just about manage to recollect enough algebra to help him. Only last week Emily had asked for some help with her maths.

'It's all stuff you've done before, Mum,' she announced with the inbuilt assumption that simply by being an adult I was on top of all such subjects.

'Yes, darling, of course,' and we sat down at the kitchen table.

'Where's your log book?'

'What's that?' she replied, puzzled. We just looked at each other and decided she would just go back to her teacher tomorrow at school. I did, however, get what I interpreted as a sympathetic note from her teacher (via Emily's homework diary) – apparently they use calculators these days and I must be as ancient as him!

Kids all off to bed, bags packed, rugby boots found and put in the boot bag where they belonged . . . I was nearly done. It's like a checklist that mothers (and some dads) have to go through every night, ranging from, 'Have I got enough milk for breakfast?' to 'I must remember to pay the water rates tomorrow,' with a thousand other things in between.

Everything ready for the morning, I sat back on the sofa and flicked the TV on, put my feet on the coffee table and drank my tea. A few moments later the phone rang and shattered my precious peace.

'Dawn, you'll never guess what? That Simon Rawlings has phoned – he wants to see you again. I told him I needed to check your availability.'

'Trish, I can't, I'm here on my own with the kids – the older girls are away, remember.' Why hadn't my reaction been, no of course I can't go, don't be silly, he's married. Why? Why had I only thought of a practical reason to not go, and not an emotional one? 'He's already said that if you aren't available he won't see anyone else, just won't bother – you obviously left an impression.'

'Tell him no, I can't. Not that I don't want to, but that I just can't.'

Trish called me back a few minutes later. 'I've got him on hold. Will you see him tomorrow at 8.30 pm, same place as before? I'll swap nights with you because you're on phone duty tomorrow?'

'Yes, tell him yes.'

How easy was that for me to say? Why was it so easy? I really did want to see Simon, wanted to be held and loved. Wait a second. Loved? Was I trying to kid myself again? He's a paying client and I am just providing a service. I willed myself to remember the truth of the situation. I slept badly that night, going through the whole rigmarole again of David's unreasonableness and how special Simon had made me feel. I tried to make it okay, to justify my actions and feelings. I failed.

By the next night I was starting to get nervous. What was I doing? Before I left I kissed Jack goodnight although he was already sound asleep. *George's Marvellous Medicine* was playing quietly on the CD player in his room so I pressed the off button – he never reached the end, he was always asleep after about five minutes. I told Victoria, 'Lights off at 8 o'clock and not a second later.' I'd told her that Nicola, the babysitter, would be up on the dot to check that all books were put away and lights were off. I kissed Victoria who was far more interested in Harry Potter than me, thinking that I needed to leave myself a note about that evening's visit from the tooth fairy. Deborah had lost a tooth and although I knew, and she knew . . . well, the tooth fairy would be calling tonight anyway. Hopefully. Because as all mummies and daddies know, sometimes the tooth fairy runs out of change or is a very forgetful fairy . . .

Deborah, Alexander and Nicola were playing Monopoly in the lounge. I reminded Nicola of the kids' bed times, told her I would be home before midnight and left them to it. Nicola was staying the night, which made life easy. She was a sixth-former at Emily's school, and lived just down the road. She could easily have gone home, but at least this way she would go to bed at a sensible time. I was going over all this stuff in my head rather than give any time or space to what I was about to do. Pretending to myself that it wasn't important, I had put jeans on again, but with a pretty top this time. Nothing special though. But who was I trying to kid as I snipped the tags off my new red and black lingerie? Surely I already had a satisfactory white cotton bra and knickers, why had I needed to go and buy this set today? I felt like a caricature from a cartoon with an angel on one shoulder and a devil on the other.

CD blaring, I drove to the hotel, Elton John assuring me that Saturday night was alright for fighting. Was it also alright for . . . ? The volume of the music and my singing perfectly drowned out every sensible thought which was vying for space inside my head. I retraced my steps, but felt a whole different set of emotions this time as I tapped on the door to Simon's room. He kissed me, passionately, deeply. Words between the kisses, 'What have you done to me?' his eyes asked the question as well as his mouth. And we made love, again and again.

'Who are you really?' he asked me. He held me close to him, as if by squeezing, the truth would have to come out. I told him my name was Dawn and that I ran the agency.

'Well, I knew you weren't Abby. I couldn't bring myself to call you that, when everything else was so . . . real.'

Why did I feel like I had known Simon forever, as if this was the most natural thing in the whole world; being in bed with him, making love, feeling so complete, so right? What the hell was wrong with me? I sat up in bed and wrapped the sheet around me. It was time to get real.

'Simon, what are we playing at? You've been using my agency for over a year. You've seen about ten different girls on about 25 occasions. I was a prostitute, and now I run an agency. Last week I came here because you're a good client and I didn't want to lose you. Tonight I came because I wanted to, and soon I will go home, back to my kids and you will go home, back to your wife and your kids, and that's it.'

'Dawn, you've consumed every waking moment of my life since you walked out of here a week ago. I can't make it go away, this feeling of wanting you, needing you. But I can't give you what you deserve, a proper relationship, and believe me, I want to. You've probably heard the same story a million times; my wife doesn't understand me and all that crap. I can't leave my kids – I just want so much for them to grow up with both of us there and then maybe one day, when the youngest is old enough, who knows . . . I've never had an affair, only ever called an agency, because I can't give anyone anything emotional.'

Then he kissed me, and every barrier, every tiny remaining drop of good sense melted away.

Simon phoned the agency number the following day but the phone was still diverted through to Trish. She called me to tell me that Simon had phoned six times, according to the call log. I cancelled the divert using the office phone, replaced the handset and turned to go back to the cooking but I only got as far as the door because the phone rang almost immediately.

'Can I take you out to dinner? Please? I want you for your mind as well as your body, you know,' he laughed down the phone. 'This Friday, please say yes – meet me at Burlington Hall. We can go in separate cars if you like, that's if you think I might turn into a mad axe-murderer. Or better still, I'll book a cab so we can have a drink and stay at the Burlington afterwards. Please?'

I was hook, line and sinkered. I suppose Simon had laid all his cards on the table, he wasn't going to leave – it just wasn't an option – so he hadn't led me up the garden path with any false promises or lies. So I said yes.

David hadn't called me and I hadn't called him, and by now it had been a month. Time was marching by and because I was busy with the agency and preoccupied with thoughts of Simon and with all the excitement and flutterings of new lust, all thoughts of David had been pushed to one side. I was tired of the misery, tired of the bickering and the rows; and Simon was so far removed from all this that I simply shut my feelings for David off.

Nicola, our babysitter, was available on Friday and would stay overnight again. I can't remember how many different outfits I tried on. Simon wouldn't tell me where we were going, only to wear something nice and not jeans. He phoned on the Thursday and asked me what my favourite colour was. 'Purple,' I said, 'deep, rich purple.'

'I knew you weren't going to be easy,' he replied very mysteriously. I drove over to the Burlington Hall, a four-star hotel in Rochester. I texted him when I'd parked and he told me to wait for him in my car.

About two minutes later he opened the car door for me, holding the most enormous bouquet of fabulous flowers, all purples and blues and whites. I'd worn a gorgeous purple dress, hoping I wasn't overdressed, and I had to laugh when the interior light from my car showed Simon was wearing a very pale purple silk tie. I was amazed at the effort he had gone to for me. Okay, it was a bunch of flowers and a tie, but that was a lot more than I was used to. Paul had never been very demonstrative and David rarely went in for grand gestures. Simon very gently propped the flowers up in the back of my car – it was one of those hand bouquets tied in water and I didn't want it to topple over.

The cab arrived and we were driven to the Deerwood Park Hotel, for the most wonderful, truly magical evening. When we arrived at the restaurant we were shown to a secluded table in the corner. A single purple rose had been placed in a crystal vase in the centre of the table – he really was trying to impress. I saw Simon wink at the maître d' who beamed back at him and nodded very slightly. Then he ordered a bottle of champagne, but in such an understated way, without any contrived flair or pretentiousness. Simon held my hand at every opportunity, told me how beautiful I was and stroked my face. The angel on my shoulder screamed in my ear that I was stupid; he probably brought all his women here – probably had a frequent diner discount! The devil stabbed the angel with his trident and she shut up for the rest of the evening.

We talked and laughed and it was perfect. The food, the wine – it was all perfect. But, like Cinderella, I had to go home. Nicola, was very responsible and very sensible but I was not about to take advantage of her good nature. We took a cab back to the Burlington and Simon asked the driver to wait. I'd already told him that I couldn't stay and he just kissed my hand and said that really wasn't what it was all about. I found my car keys, took the flowers from my car and put them in the back of the cab. Simon paid the driver and asked me what time I wanted to be picked up tomorrow to retrieve my car. Was there anything he hadn't thought of? He kissed me and I kissed him back, really wanting to spend the night with him, but I knew there would be another time, very soon.

The following day he texted me, then rang to say how much he'd enjoyed himself and hoped I had picked my car up without any problems. Simon ran his own business, very expensive bespoke kitchen installations, £50,000 and more a time, so he had to see clients in the evening, and travel long distances. One of these was booked in for early Tuesday evening so Simon would be free from about 7.00 pm, and he asked if we could do something then. Was this what I really wanted, someone who could 'get away' from time to time, someone who could sneak the odd night here and there?

The phone wasn't terribly busy that night so I was pottering about in the kitchen in between the phone calls. Martin phoned at about 11.30 pm – a call I knew had to come, but I was dreading it nonetheless. I'd talked with Trish and Paula about Jenny de-livering the packages because we didn't know which of us would have to speak to Martin, but I was so relieved it was me. I hated putting the other two in the position of having to lie to someone like him. After much discussion the girls and I had come up with what we hoped and prayed would be a plausible story.

'Hello Princess, is my Jenny coming to see me tonight then?' he asked.

'Martin, sweetness, how are you? Jenny – look, slight problem. I'll get straight to the point: unfortunately she's picked up something rather nasty.' I could hear Martin swallowing hard, and I wished I could have seen his face.

'Right . . . okay, well . . . I'll give it a miss tonight actually, I could probably do with the sleep . . . too much work, you know how it is. I'll be in touch soon.'

Well, that let Jenny off the hook but what about all the other girls? Martin was lucky with Jenny because she was so naïve. I now had a massive problem. I knew he wouldn't want to see

Jenny ever again, which was great, but what if he rang and wanted someone else? I certainly didn't want anyone else doing deliveries for him, but I'd heard what he could be like if he was crossed. If I suddenly refused to send anyone to him, he'd know that I was onto him – that I'd had a look inside one of his packages to Josh – and then Jenny and I would both be in big trouble. I had a flash of inspiration about half an hour later as I was pulling the washing out of the machine and pushing it into the tumble dryer. It was risky but I would try to arrange an 'accidental' meeting. Yes, I knew exactly what to do. I shut the dryer door assertively, doing my best to ignore the apprehension that was also lurking.

The following morning I collared Debbie in the car park at school. As we both wound our windows down, the situation reminded me of a second-rate spy movie. 'Debbie, meet me at Al Forno at 12.30 today. It's really important – you have to be there.'

'Hmm, let me see, I was going to clean the bathrooms today and then start on the washing. So . . . lunch at our favourite Italian or scrubbing the underwear worn by the five men in my life? Difficult one. Let me see . . .'

'Shut up, you silly mare! I'll see you there at 12.30, and I mean 12.30 for once in your life. Don't be late!'

'Bossy old bag,' she muttered as she drove off.

We met in Blue Boar Lane car park opposite the restaurant and walked up there together. Paolo, one of the owners, kissed us both amidst his trademark compliment, '*Bella, bella!*', and found us a quiet table in the corner. Sure enough, Martin was there surrounded by his 'associates'. When he saw Debbie and me he came over to say hello. Unfortunately many people knew who he was, and the last thing I wanted was to be associated with him in any way. Still, I thought this was the best course of action, for me and for all the girls who worked at the agency. Martin's children went to the same school as ours and hopefully to anyone looking on we were all just parents of children in the same class who had happened to bump into each other. The restaurant was always quite busy and had a bit of a reputation as being the place to be seen. Martin Brookman always ate there as did everyone else who was, or thought they were, a 'face'. The food was fantastic and the owners had a knack of making you feel really special. The kids loved Al Forno and were always made a great fuss of.

'So glad to have run into you, Martin. Actually, I do need a quick word,' I said, trying to look very serious. Debbie, realising that this was her cue, excused herself to the ladies, leaving us alone. 'A couple of my girls have attracted the attention, through no fault of their own, of our dear friends the police. So it might be a good idea to . . .'

'Oh yes, absolutely.' His eyes made it very clear he understood. 'I'll be in touch. Lovely to see you.' As he left our table he leaned down for a final word in my ear. 'Thanks for that, much appreciated. Lunch on my tab, I'll tell Paolo. Well done, Dawn. Good to know who my friends are.' He kissed me on both cheeks and rejoined his party, leaving a waft of aftershave and an uncomfortable silence.

Debbie had only just returned. 'I don't want to know – really, I don't – but is everything okay? You wanted to see him here, didn't you? This wasn't an accident, bumping into him I mean. I hope you know what you're doing.'

'That depends what you mean by okay. I think I've successfully dodged a nasty problem. But I'm pretty sure an even bigger one is about to hit me.'

Chapter Twenty

Simon called me a few days later and asked if I would like to go out with him again. 'No pressure, but I'll jump off Rochester Bridge if you say no,' he joked. There was never any danger of that because I said yes instantly. He said he knew a really nice restaurant in Blackheath and asked if I was free on Friday. A neat swap with Paula and then, yes, I was free.

The kids were going to stay with Paul at his parents' house straight from school, so I didn't even have to worry about a babysitter. Simon offered to pick me up and I hesitated because, despite thinking that he was Casanova and George Clooney rolled into one, I was still attempting to be vaguely sensible. Picking upon my hesitation over giving him my address, Simon pointed out that I knew that he was married, where he lived, his home phone number, and he was under no illusions that he had rather a lot at stake here. So I gave him my address and he picked me up at 7.30 pm.

I felt as if I'd known Simon forever, which I know sounds corny, but I really did. The Blackheath restaurant was indeed fabulous. I knew what was happening and just couldn't help myself. I didn't ask him how he could do this but his wife seemed to know he was out and didn't appear to mind. I just enjoyed his company while we were together. I shut off everything, just accepted what he told me about his relationship with his wife and believed him. When we drove back down the A2 several hours later and then parked outside my house, I asked if he wanted to come in for a coffee – another fabulous expression which really means a multitude of other thoughts and desires. I took Simon's hand, led him to my bedroom and eventually woke early in the morning to find him kissing me tenderly and saying goodbye.

'I have to go now. Can I come back this evening?' I'll give you six guesses as to my response . . .

The following week, I'd arranged to meet a couple of girl-friends in The Velvet Rooms for lunch. As I am so often late, Kirsty and Maggie were already there. About five seconds after I had sat down, a bottle of very nice wine and three glasses appeared just as Kirsty was about to go to the bar and order some drinks. Before I could point out that we hadn't ordered anything yet, the waiter indicated my new best friend, Martin Brookman, who was standing discreetly at the very end of the bar.

Not really sure what to do, I went over to Martin and said thank you. He gave me a peck on the cheek, said it was his pleasure and hoped we would be staying for lunch. It was lovely to see me again etc, etc – all in flamboyant tones. The problem was, Martin liked to hold court but very rarely communicated directly with anyone – he usually sent one of his minions. Now it seemed he was trying to give me a special and personal thank you for my supposed tip-off. But, the last thing I needed was public recognition from the local hoodlum!

Kirsty and Maggie were both speechless when I came back. 'Girls, it's not what it looks – can we just get that straight?' Having known both of them for years trust was a given, so I explained about the mess Jenny had found herself in and my subsequent involvement. Maggie winced and Kirsty pulled that face you make when you bite on a lemon. It really was that bad. I felt uncomfortable but, again, the risk of offending Martin was too great so we stayed put and had lunch.

The following afternoon I met Kirsty briefly in Rochester and just had time for a quick coffee and cake before picking up the kids up from school. I really thought she was joking at first but then saw it for myself – as we walked the length of the high street to get to the coffee shop, a few people nodded in our direction and then continued their conversations with furtive or backwards glances. I was horrified to realise that people were obviously speculating as to my connections with Martin. Rochester is a small place but full of people who think they really are somebody. I was really trying to be the opposite – anonymous. No chance of that now.

I parked in the school car park and found Debbie. We both had kids doing clubs after school so we sat around talking while we waited for them to finish. The other kids, still in their uniforms, passed the time by playing football on the tennis court.

We chatted about the upcoming school revue. This year, the PTA mothers were performing their own interpretation of Liberty X's 'Sexy' dressed as cleaners, although some bright spark had the idea that it would be funny to include someone dressed up as a French maid. And guess who had been volunteered to do that! Actually, it was all very funny to start with, all feather dusters and marigolds, but then the problems started. Debbie told me that one of the self-righteous mothers had objected to the chairlady of the PTA that she didn't think that 'someone like me' should be allowed to be a part of the revue. I was very upset.

We were only a couple of weeks away from the actual performance and I was furious. Why are people so harsh, so judgemental, when they know so few of the facts? If I were recruiting escorts from the lower sixth they might justifiably had something to say but I ran an agency that prioritised the girls' safety and didn't see them as a mere source of income. Otherwise, I was just a mum at the school who made cakes when asked and helped out at the PTA. I decided to ignore the gossip and not let this group of women get to me. I stuck with the rehearsals, but they were a quick in-and-out for me. I had no desire to stay on, to give anyone ammunition or target practice.

I saw Simon a few times during the couple of weeks. Every time he arrived on my doorstep, every time I kissed him, I told myself just how stupid I was being. We went out for dinner or he came over at 10-ish and then we went to bed, with a 5.00 am goodbye. Every time I saw him, I knew he was right about us; it was wrong. I wanted him so badly, the whole thing, I wanted him lock, stock and barrel – but he had been honest right from the start and never misled me. So I told him that because it was so good, it had to end – he was right – I couldn't handle it any more.

As I deleted his number from my phone I cried for myself, for what might have been and for the wonderful times we had shared. I really did feel like my heart was breaking, and the noise inside my head was like glass shattering into a million pieces all day long. I had broken my own golden rule about getting involved with a client and was left feeling broken-hearted and full of self-pity.

I made my normal round of Monday morning phone calls, which now took so long due to the sheer number of the girls, drivers and male escorts. I had to take enormous care with each call, relying on my notes on the personal circumstances of each of the escorts and in some cases the drivers too. Girls like Lynda, for example, whose husband had no idea what she was up to. It wasn't always convenient for her to talk, so I had to ring back later or wait for her to have some privacy to call me.

My notes for each girl included her cover story so that when I called Sally for example, if one of her kids answered the phone and Mummy wasn't there, I'd leave a message from Dawn, the bar manager at the nightclub where Sally was apparently a barmaid three times a week. And if her husband answered I'd find him asking me how things were, if the club was busy and if there was any chance of a few more shifts for his wife, as he was out of work. And so it went on. It was like playing a part in several soap operas simultaneously.

Sally wasn't the only one whose family thought she worked in a club, but many others used the 'care worker on call' ruse; responding to emergency call-outs via the SOS pendants that the elderly or infirm wear around their necks. That was a good one because it accounted for the extra miles on the car and any carelessly discarded petrol receipts. I had to make sure I was familiar with each girl's cover story, just in case. Obviously the last thing I wanted was to drop anyone in it.

Marie was home when I called her and picked up straight away. She gave me her availability and we chatted about her sons and their feelings towards her now that some time had passed. Her daughter-in-law had fought Marie's corner all the way, which had brought them very close. Darren was still barely talking to his mother, indeed he was only just about managing to be civil, but it was an improvement from his initial reaction. Marie had something to tell me and I had a vague suspicion I knew what it was. 'I've saved enough! Finally, finally I've done it!' The relief, the joy in her voice was almost tangible. 'With the equity in my house here added to my savings, I'm off to sunny Spain!' Dreams do come true, I reminded myself, and congratulated her.

An estate agent was going to value the house at the end of the week, and in a couple of weeks' time she planned to take a long weekend in Malaga to have a look around. I knew she'd been to some of those Spanish property exhibitions they run at out-of-town hotels and I was delighted for her. Marie wanted to keep working for a while, just a couple of nights a week, in case the house took longer to sell than anticipated. She'd already handed her notice in at work and she didn't want to burn all her bridges at once. The boys would eventually come round, especially once she had moved on and had settled in Spain. I could just see her working behind a bar, maybe doing a little waitressing, smiling and content.

Chapter Twenty-One

I drove to Gatwick to collect Emily and Alice and I was really looking forward to seeing them. They finally came through arrivals, exhausted but nut-brown and all smiles, and it was lovely to have them back. They were half asleep as we drove home but desperate to tell me all about it – the food, the hotel, the beaches, the poverty, the mad taxi driver. Their excitement was wonderful to see and I was so glad they'd made the trip to India. Over the next few days I heard all about the visit to the tea plantation, the children they'd seen begging and the contrasts of a culture so different from our own. I now knew that Emily was going to try to achieve world peace, end poverty and feed every hungry child at the very least! Meanwhile I would carry on feeding my six.

Easter was fast approaching and the school Easter egg hunt loomed. I sat with Debbie at a very stuffy PTA meeting one

Tuesday morning. We ploughed through all the usual, such as who would help make the tea at open day, until we reached the last item on the agenda; the Easter egg hunt. Kerry, our chair, explained that the children would hunt the school grounds for not-very-well-hidden coloured discs and exchange them for small chocolate eggs. In previous years the eggs had been donated or discounted, but this year the PTA would have to buy them because the source of the donation had ceased. We would still have the Easter egg hunt but it would probably run at a loss.

I had an idea, but didn't like to say anything to Kerry until I had called in a favour. One of our long-standing regular clients was the manager of a local branch of a rather well-known supermarket chain. Ian only liked to see one young lady in particular but was generally in the position where he could only book at very short notice; I had often already allocated the bookings and then had to so some serious swapping around. I presumed his wife went out unplanned or something along those lines. He knew it was a pain to chop and change bookings but it couldn't be helped. I called Ian on his mobile and left a very ambiguous message. He called me back from his office when he had a little privacy and I made my request. It turned out they had a charity slush fund and he'd be only too glad to be of assistance. There would be £120 of vouchers at the customer service desk for my attention.

I found Kerry in the car park the following morning and told her that one of my clients had very kindly agreed to donate the Easter eggs. She was really very pleased. Obviously it was much better for the school fund to run events at a profit and the Easter egg hunt would now do so. It just remained for me to collect the vouchers and choose the eggs.

Around this time David broke the silence at last with a birthday card for me. He must have put it through the door very early that morning on his way to work. At about 11.00 am Scooby went ballistic, standard procedure when anyone knocked on the door. I opened it to find a tiny woman engulfed by the most stunning arrangement of red and yellow roses I had ever seen. A dozen of each, long-stemmed with the most perfect heads, just ready to unfurl. The guilt I felt about what happened with Simon had been overpowering enough when I opened David's beautiful card, but now each of these stunning roses screamed 'Traitor!' at me. David always bought me red and yellow roses; red for love and yellow for friendship.

I felt enormously guilty, totally undeserving, and unsure of my feelings towards David. I had loved him from the first second I'd seen him years ago. But look at what I'd done, we'd had a row and I had become all moonstruck over an unavailable client. I didn't deserve his love and he certainly didn't deserve my lies and deceit. I rang him to say thank you for the card and the flowers. David had tears in his voice, he said he missed me, he loved me and he wanted to meet up to sort things out. I couldn't cope with him being so loving when all I felt was guilt. So I said no.

I went for a walk that evening with Scooby down by the river. It was about 10.00 pm but very well lit along that stretch of the park. David was ringing my mobile but I just ignored it and eventually switched it off. I couldn't work out how I felt about him. Why had it been so easy to be with Simon in the first instance? Was it really just a business decision? Actually, that very first time, it was. And Simon had wanted sex from me – well, anybody really – that first time. The difference between sex and love was that when you loved someone both physically and emotionally, using both your heart and your body, you gave a little of yourself each time. When I was totally honest with myself, I realised that Simon didn't ever take any of me; we had no depth, no time to know each other whereas David owned me – heart, body and soul.

Scooby ran towards a shape in the distance and I knew it was David, even though the figure was too far away for me to make out any features. I knew it was him because he was the only person who would know where to find me. He's the only person who has ever found me. We picked up where we'd left off and things pretty much went back to normal. Every row leaves a scar but time is a great healer and bad memories fade – they don't disappear, but they do fade.

Sharon had been working virtually every night, telling Colin that she needed the money to give them a head start when they eventually got together. Colin didn't book her through the agency now – he couldn't afford to. Unfortunately Sharon had lost the buyer for her house, a last-minute change of heart, which badly upset her plans for a new life. With things in turmoil, all plans on hold, Sharon reduced the asking price of her house in an attempt to stave off Colin's persistence. It wasn't long before she found another buyer. The sale progressed smoothly this time, and she actually managed to exchange contracts. The sigh of relief she breathed the night she told me was huge.

It was a weeknight and I was taking the bookings. Sharon had an hour to kill before she made her way over to Cuxton to see a client. We sat in the office and I'd never seen her looking so tired – haggard even. She seemed to have aged so much in the past six months and I was sure it was all the stress of being involved with Colin. It wasn't the money that he had bailed her out with, and the nagging possibility that one day he might go to a solicitor or even the police and force her to give it back, although that was bad enough. The real problem was the fact that Colin seemed to know so much about her. He constantly dropped bits of information he's gleaned about her life into the conversation – the ages of her kids or what schools they went to – that scared her the most. His veiled threats, his taunting, and the power he held over her; his knowledge of her parallel lives. Colin was the only person, other than me, who knew what Sharon did, how she fed her kids and paid the mortgage. He left sentences unfinished. 'Wouldn't it be a disaster if they all found out . . . ?' Sharon used every excuse in the book to avoid seeing him but they ran out after a while and she really was stuck with him.

Of course he would want to go out with her, to a restaurant or the cinema but Sharon hated being seen in public with him. David and I were sitting in a restaurant next to the multi-screen cinema complex in Rochester one evening, having a meal before going to see a film, when who should sit at the next table but

Sharon and Colin. I kicked David under the table and stopped him before he could acknowledge Sharon, whispering to him that he was to just to ignore her and pretend he didn't know her. Sharon looked around the whole time she was there, desperately praying that she didn't bump into anyone she knew, wondering how she would ever explain who Colin was. And there was Colin, desperate to meet her friends and announce to the world that this was the woman he intended to marry. In four weeks' time the house would be sold and Sharon and her kids would be headed for a different life in another country, free of her past and of stupid mistakes like Colin. But for the time being Sharon worked, saved, worried and prayed.

The rehearsals for the revue were going well, although I was still smarting over the remarks about me and my business from some of the other mums.

Interestingly, their husbands reacted rather differently. I probably did dress a bit more glamorously than their partners, but you can tell when a man looks at you that bit too long, with extra curiosity, daring themselves to meet your eye. That was at school. But I also bumped into several of them in town. Away from their wives they could even afford to risk an exchange, 'Dawn, how are you? Better be careful, mustn't be seen with the likes of you,' frequently accompanied by a wink. Many of them had personal experience of the world I worked in, of that I was sure. Those that didn't had probably thought about it, and seeing me could well have been a sort of trigger, reminding them of this other daring, forbidden world. On some level, I could understand why some of the mothers perceived me as a threat, especially if their marriages were on shaky ground. I did feel sorry for them, but it still hurt when they made me the focus of all their fears.

The revue was on the following Saturday night and our turn was the last act of the first half. I took the children and sat them with some friends. Debbie and I disappeared to get changed with a couple of acts still in front of ours – I definitely was not looking forward to this and just wanted it all to be over. I put the French maid's outfit on, complete with black tights, black shoes with four-inch heels, black rubber gloves and a pink feather duster. Amidst cheers and catcalls, we danced and I have never felt as relieved as I did when I finally came off that stage. One of the mothers looked at me as we were changing and, out of nowhere, sheepishly said she was sorry for the silly misunderstanding. I just looked at her and turned away. I know I should have accepted her apology, but did she not realise how much hurt she had caused me? I might have appeared tough on the outside, but it was really just an act. The gossip was so malicious; did these women ever stop to think that I might have feelings? Had they ever bothered to think how it would affect my children if their children passed the rumours on to mine? It was unthinkable.

The following weekend Kirsty, her boyfriend, Zubin, and her kids all came over for Sunday lunch. David's kids were staying over this weekend too, so there had been 13 for lunch, which was hectic, but after lunch was delightfully relaxed. Zubin was from India and was interested to hear about Emily and Alice's recent trip. The girls had bought home bags and bags of different spices and teas, and Zubin was in the kitchen with me, making chai, just like his mum made. Very soon a fabulous smell was coming from a saucepan on the hob as he added tiny amounts of wonderful ingredients. When it was finally ready, Zubin, Kirsty and I each had a sample of the spicy sweet tea. It was delicious and he wrote down all that he had used to make it. I loved days like this. Friends over, a few bottles of wine, a lovely meal, all the kids playing happily, running in and out of the house, chasing the dog. At times like this I really believed that I had found the Enid Blyton life that I so longed for.

The Tuesday visit to the bank had come around and thankfully I'd got there with the money from the girls before the lunchtime crush. I was sitting at the corner table, filling in the paying-in slip, minding my own business. Though I'd done this countless times before, there was something about having a fairly large amount of cash next to me that always kept a part of my brain on alert. Or maybe it was the feeling that even though there was nothing illegal about the way it was earned, the way it was acquired still made it somehow more fragile, likely to be snatched back.

Which is why I very quickly picked up that someone was inside my personal space, at my shoulder. And no sooner had I realised this than a porridgy voice straight out of a gangster film said, 'Hello darling. Your friend Martin would like a little meeting.' I hadn't even turned my head round. 'He'll pick you up at ten tomorrow morning. You're not busy, are you?'

Well, if I had been, I was hardly about to say 'yes'. As I fully turned round, all I could see was the back of a blue Crombie coat and a square neck with more creases than my ironing pile.

A moment's thought and I knew what this was going to be about. One of the girls had seen a client who decided in his infinite stupidity to tell her details of a drugs delivery. Not times and places, thank goodness, otherwise that would have put me in a very difficult situation. But he did tell her how it was arriving, packed into copper tubing. This kind of information was not stuff that Martin wanted flying about, and the girl couldn't wait to share the problem with me. The safest course of action had been for me to pass the gist of it on to Martin – if it ever got to him that we knew this guy was a 'leaky bucket' and hadn't passed it on, things for the agency and for me would have become very difficult, not to say dangerous. Going to the police wasn't an option given who I was dealing with.

The next morning one of Martin's associates picked me up. As familiar streets and shops went by I watched from the inside of the blacked-out windows, envying the simple life of every shopper I saw.

Martin was very much on the case. The client in question ran the haulage company and future deals were now in jeopardy. So there I was, being asked what had been said about what and to whom. I tried to reassure him with answers that were truthful but not alarming. How could I make it clear that, of course we were always on his side, but that mine was not like his business, let alone part of it? And all this with another parent from school.

Maybe he could live comfortably being part of these two worlds but for me the meeting couldn't end soon enough.

'She's a good girl is she, Dawn?'

I knew what he meant by 'good'. 'Oh yes, Martin. I don't think she's the one you've got to worry about.'

Later that day, and trying my best not to think about Martin, I went to the supermarket and found Ian, the supermarket manager and client who had offered the Easter eggs to the school, standing by the customer-service desk. I had never actually met him before but as he was wearing a badge with his name on, he was hard to miss. I introduced myself and with a wink he told me he was only too pleased to support such a worthy cause. He gave me the vouchers and asked me to sign for them. As he put them in my hand he gave it a squeeze and with another neatly delivered wink asked me to call him and let him know how the event went. An assistant found a trolley for me, and without having to scrabble for a pound I went off to buy 300 Easter eggs.

I counted them up and threw in a few spares just in case. To save the bother of loading and unloading them, and also keep them away from little fingers and mouths I thought it best to not take the eggs home. I drove home to my usual round of chores before collecting the kids from school. Tomorrow was the Easter egg hunt and I needed to get all this chocolate out of my car and into somewhere cool. So once I arrived at school, Kerry helped me unload and carry all the eggs to the school kitchens.

Debbie was waving at me, big grin, and full of news.

'Boy, is your name mud!'

So, what was new? 'Go on then, tell me what's going on. What have I done now?'

Debbie had been accosted by one of the mothers who'd asked her if it was true one of the agency's clients had donated the Easter eggs. On finding out that they indeed had, they were up in arms, and had demanded that the eggs be discarded and replacements found. Obviously, Ian's eggs were somehow tainted and unclean. Give me strength! Kerry certainly didn't seem to have a problem with where the eggs had come from, and as far as I was concerned I really couldn't see that anyone could possibly object. Ian was a contact through my business and had made a generous donation on behalf of his company. That really was all there was to it.

Despite only being the end of March, it really was a lovely day for the hunt. Sunny with blue skies, and you could smell the promise of warmth to come in the air. Some of the yummy mummies had volunteered to disperse the coloured discs around the grounds for the children to find but Debbie and I decided to go for our weekly shop and back to her house. Debbie hates housework and does as little as possible. She found space in the cupboards for her shopping while I stood for an hour and did her ironing. With her the vast quantities of ironing, and her hate of doing it, her piles of washing were forever building up. Me, I can't just sit there and look at it – it's a bit of an obsession.

Debbie and I trundled off to school at the appointed hour and found our children. In amongst the bags of eggs I had given Kerry, there was a special Caramac egg for Victoria as chocolate is full of caffeine and therefore out of bounds. The school bell was ringing as Debbie and I arrived and moments later the first child appeared, followed by a steady stream of excited kids, hardly needing all the additives they were about to consume. My kids dumped their satchels, PE kits, lunch boxes and all the other paraphernalia that accompanies four primary-school children on the last day of term into the boot of my car. Amazingly well prepared for once, I gave each pair of grubby little mitts a 50-pence piece and off they went to join in the Easter egg hunt. The idea was to find five discs to get an egg – hopefully it would take the children about ten minutes and all the running around would wear them out. No chance of that. Have you ever tried to wear out a nine-year-old? Impossible.

Debbie and I sat on a bench with a couple of other friends who just accepted me as the mum of their children's friends. We watched the kids dashing about, looking forward to their rewards. They'd heard all the rumours. One said she'd heard I was still working myself, the other asked for a job! The clique clucked past us with what I imagine they thought were very disapproving looks, but which only succeeded in making us all laugh.

Our children returned triumphant, already tucking into their various trophies, traces of chocolate smeared across faces and on fingers. We piled into the car, looking forward to the Easter holidays, complete with projects on ancient Greece as well as holiday diaries to fill in, but most of all grateful for the luxury of not having to get up at 7.00 am.

Chapter Twenty-Two

I stretched and yawned in bed. David hadn't woken me up when he left that morning at 7.00 am, not properly anyway. I had a vague recollection of his kisses and a whispered, 'See you tonight, I love you,' before I rolled over for another decadent hour.

It was the first day of the Easter holidays. So lovely not to have to rush around chasing the kids into the car before I did my usual race to school, arriving right as the bell rang for morning roll-call. I looked at the clock, registering it was nearly 9.00 am, and wondered how on earth the kids had managed not to fight and argue loudly enough to wake me up.

I found my dressing gown and slippers and went downstairs to greet the usual morning devastation which accompanies my brood. Emily and Alice were still in bed – not really that much of a surprise. Victoria and Jack were eating toast and bowls of porridge that Deborah very kindly made for them. I ignored the kitchen, making a mental note to come back to the mess later on, and headed to the utility room, where the washing machine was beeping at me. On autopilot I reached for a laundry basket and pulled the wet washing out of the machine, unlocked the back door, let Scooby out for a wee and hung the washing on the line. It was a ritual I had performed thousands of times, muttering the same things as I was left with odd socks and broke yet another peg.

I had arranged to take the kids and meet up with Debbie and her kids at Shorne Wood Country Park at 2.00 pm, and was so grateful for the lovely weather. We would take Scooby for a long walk; hopefully he wouldn't jump in the river and roll in the mud. Then we'd go to the café for ice creams and a coffee before heading home for dinner. I had the usual Monday morning ahead of me – phoning the girls, planning rosters – but I'd get most of it taken care of before we went out. I called the kids, who emerged in various states of undress, and ordered showers, dressing, bedrooms tidied, dirty washing found and general preparations to enable us to leave the house on time.

I loaded up my slow cooker with all the ingredients for a spaghetti bolognese and five minutes later dinner was under way, albeit slowly. The washing machine was on, dishwasher whirring away and I was on my way upstairs for a shower and to find something to wear to the park. I bribed the kids with promises that I would think about a trip to Thorpe Park this holiday – a very carefully worded bribe – and they started their homework.

When it was time to leave, I herded children and dog into the car. It was still a bright sunny day and the kids were full up with lunch and excitement. We arrived a little early and, as we were swapping trainers for wellies and trying to control Scooby, who was going mad in anticipation of a swimming trip, Debbie pulled up in the bay next to me.

The kids climbed trees, played football, timed themselves on their make-shift assault course and played hide and seek. From the expression on her face, I could tell Debbie had something on her mind and I thought she would probably work around to it after all the usual talk about partners, kids, her mother, mother-in-law, etc, as women do. We sat watching the kids on the monkey bars and swings when Debbie finally broached the subject. Debbie had a 13-year-old son, Daniel, in the senior school. Daniel had told her that some of the boys in his class had been teasing him about his mum being friendly with me because I ran a 'brothel' and looked after prostitutes. This had happened in the last week of term, and Debbie had wanted to wait for the holidays before she told me. She must have wanted to spare me the upset of having to wait at the gates with the mothers spreading such gossip to their children. Thankfully, Daniel was fairly level-headed, had just said something dismissive and not risen to any bait. Apparently the matter had been dropped but with teenage boys, the subject was bound to come up again.

Words can't be found to describe how sick I felt. Poor Daniel, being subjected to taunting because of his mum's friendship with me. And Debbie, how awful for her to have her son put through this. She saw how upset I was for them both and just brushed it aside. 'Don't be silly, Dawn, it's okay . . . nothing but a load of spiteful gossip. It'll pass.' I wished I had her confidence but somehow I couldn't share her feelings in any way. Debbie called Daniel over and I said how sorry I was about what he'd gone through. Daniel was fine, and said he'd just wanted to punch the boys but didn't want any more demerits right now! Reluctantly, the kids came off the swings and we all walked back to the cars, the kids muddy, hungry as always . . . and me? I was extremely apprehensive.

I plugged the phone into the socket in the office at about 6.30 pm that night and diverted the calls through to Paula. I was so relieved not to be taking the bookings as I had a killer headache and couldn't help thinking about my children, and what nasty stories they may already have heard and not told me about. We made plans for the following day – a trip to the library to find some books on ancient Greece for Victoria and Jack and then Alexander wanted to go to Rochester Castle. We had climbed the castle so many times but I suppose when you're a kid it's exciting every time.

After hunting for library cards and overdue books, we were ready to go. The day was quite chilly but not a drop of rain in sight, so we decided to walk to Rochester. As we crossed the bridge into town I hoped the books weren't going to be massive reference ones, as I'd have a slightly less happy band of brothers and sisters on the journey home. Once we were there, the kids chose their books, we printed out some information from the internet and the librarian very kindly said we could leave our pile of books and pick them up on the way home. One problem neatly avoided.

We left the library and walked down to the baker to buy lunch. It was there again, the feeling that people were looking at me, or was I just being paranoid? No, it was happening. People whom I now knew were 'faces'; people I wouldn't have wanted to know under any circumstances. These small-time criminals and shady figures were probably thinking of me as one of their own, showing their solidarity with me against the system with subtle nods in my direction. As I walked past a group of them sitting outside a pub, a very well-known heavy winked at me and smiled at the kids.

'Lovely day!'

This was a nightmare. How could anyone want to be a part of this world? Was I really that naïve to think that that these worlds would never collide? From wanting to run a successful business to support the kids I was now being acknowledged by the local drug dealers, fixers and hoodlums. I suppose I should have realised from the beginning that the connections between the criminal world and the sex industry run deep and that in many people's minds they were part of the same world. When I set up the agency, I was so convinced I could escape those associations being levelled at me by running my business honestly and by keeping my head down. It never occurred to me that I'd find myself in this situation.

I smiled vacuously at the man as I took the children into the bakery. I tried with all my will to ignore what was really happening while we bought sausage rolls, doughnuts and cartons of Ribena before crossing the road to buy bananas and grapes from the greengrocer. We sat on the steps of the bandstand at the castle gardens, feeding the pigeons with the leftovers, wiped our greasy hands on tissues and clattered up the metal steps to the ticket office.

On a clear day the view from the top of the castle is stunning. The river snakes around the estuary and Rochester Cathedral looks magnificent. The kids ran about, shouting and playing, shooting imaginary arrows and pouring boiling oil onto invisible invading armies. Their lives were so simple, so uncomplicated, and that was how I wanted it to stay. Their happiness, stability and security were vitally important, but how was I going to keep all that together with the way things were now? How was I going to protect my children from all the bad things in the world when the bad things were on our very own doorstep?

We walked home, having collected the library books. We waved to friends who ran a jeweller's next to the library and I clung to the familiarity, the warmth I had always felt in Rochester; at the same time I hated the other side of the equation, the association with Martin Brookman.

I took the bookings that night. England were playing some European team in a Cup game, and as much as I couldn't stand football, it was important to know because, whilst we hardly took any calls during big matches, there was generally a deluge of calls an hour or two after the final whistle. Several of the girls had bookings which had been arranged beforehand, and those who didn't were taking advantage of the football and not starting work until about 10.00 pm.

I gave the children their dinner fairly early and waited for David to come home so I could eat with him. Amazingly, I only had to answer the phone twice during the whole meal, which was a lovely change. The third time the phone rang it was Sharon, distraught. She had a booking at 9.00 pm in Crawley and was on her way over. However, she had spotted Colin in her rear-view mirror as she pulled out of the road she lived in. Now she was on the M26 and Colin was still a few cars behind her. What was he doing? After trying to calm her down, I told her to keep going until she reached a service station. She was to get out and go to the toilet, compose herself and see what Colin did. If she stayed there for 15 minutes or so she would still have plenty of time to reach her booking on time.

I didn't want to say anything to Sharon to make her feel any worse, but I had a feeling that Colin was making sure she really was working and hadn't disappeared, which of course is exactly what she soon planned to do. She'd told him that the house sale would be completing two weeks after it actually was, which would give her plenty of time to go. I also thought Colin wasn't quite as gullible as Sharon had first thought and, as things were dragging on, perhaps he was checking up on her. I was weary of this, the constant problems, the ringing of the phone – intrusive, yet vital to the business – and I was beginning to resent it all. Sharon calmed down and did as I suggested. Colin followed her all night and she never said a word to him about it.

We spoke on the phone the next day and, as her first booking that night had already been made for Dartford, Sharon asked if

I was free and if she could call in on the way. When she came in, she looked even more worn out than the last time I'd seen her. I told her I was really worried that Colin might have an inkling that she was going to do a flit and cause her all sorts of problems, so she agreed to be extra careful and make sure that everything really was set up so she could just disappear. She'd set the date to leave, rented a villa for six months and arranged storage for a few pieces of furniture.

Sharon had told everyone, including the buyers of her house, that she was renting a house in the area, a smaller house because two of her children would no longer be living with her. The rest she had agreed to sell to her buyers. She was going to pack the car as full as possible, drive down to Spain, unload and try to make the villa feel like home. A week later she'd fly back to England, collect the kids and the last remaining things, buy a new mobile phone and be free of Colin forever. In theory it was simple and hopefully Colin would never find her, if he was inclined to look. She had done well from the sale of her house so would have plenty of breathing space once she was settled in to the beautiful villa she had shown me photos of. I envied Sharon for her escape and the anonymity of her new life. Three weeks and then freedom, she said. I didn't know how she was going to last for three weeks with all the pressure she had put herself under, but somehow I knew she would find the strength to cope.

Chapter Twenty-Three

*K*ids hate doing projects through school holidays and, as a parent speaking from bitter experience, I hate doing them as well! The project on ancient Greece was no different. As much as I love the stories and even studied Greek literature at school, it is such a chore to convince your child of the benefits of completing the project. After a week of cajoling, persuading, helping and finally resorting to threats, Victoria's project was finished, out of the way and literally in the bag, ready for the new term. We had a day out in London to celebrate, which felt so fabulously normal. We went shopping in Covent Garden, went on the London Eye and ate at the Rainforest Café. Later we met up with Debbie and went to see a film.

The next day, I was hanging out the washing with the wind whipping at the sheets when Alexander and Deborah came into the garden. 'Mum, look at this,' he said, handing me his mobile.

Thinking it was a silly joke or daft picture I finished what I was doing, just glancing at the screen, then did a double take when I realised what it actually said. The text message read, 'My mum says your mum is a prostitute.' Deborah and Alexander just looked at me, waiting for an explanation, for me to say something – anything – but what could – or should – I say to them? God, kids could be so cruel.

I phoned Debbie and Kirsty and they were both over in a flash. Debbie brought her kids and we watched as they trundled off to the park with Scooby in tow. Kirsty turned up with her kids soon after and, once they were all playing in a manner that didn't require constant intervention, we were able to talk.

The text had come from a girl at Alexander's school, who just happened to be the daughter of one of the self-righteous set. This woman was hardcore – she wanted me hung, drawn and quartered. When I first read the text I just willed it to disappear, which of course it didn't. I did try to just laugh it off with the kids, saying that people were horrible, weren't they? Alexander had an idea what the word meant but Deborah certainly didn't. I wasn't sure if they'd had a discussion of their own before showing the message to me so I tried to dismiss it then changed the subject. They seemed to forget about it all in the chaos that surrounded Debbie's arrival with three of her boisterous children.

What a mess. First, my supposed involvement with Martin Brookman, and now my children were being exposed to my past. I would have to tell the kids at some stage because far too many people knew, but at a time when they were old enough to under-stand and form their own opinions. Not now, not at this age; they were far too young. I knew that the situation was of my own doing, after all, nobody forced me to be a prostitute, but having made that decision surely my children didn't deserve this? I have very broad shoulders and felt I would just have to cope with whatever was thrown at me. But the idea of an adult actually dis-cussing something like this with their child, or even within earshot of their child, is incomprehensible to me, no matter how much they disapprove of my choices and actions. If someone wants to have a go at me that's fine, but leave my children out of it. My kids were not fair game, and I felt as guilty as hell for the position they were now in. I didn't want my children going back to school and being teased because of me.

So I made the decision there and then to move, to do what Sharon was doing, to become anonymous and run away. I wanted to be able to walk down the road again without people thinking that they knew who I was, what I was; I wanted my children to be able to go to school without fear of being teased or bullied. Debbie admitted that she hadn't told me the full extent of the gossip and the rumours, never thinking that anyone would be callous enough to tell their children, even indirectly. But if I ran away, where on earth would I go? What about the business? What about David? Alexander was due to go to the grammar school next year, Emily would be taking her GCSEs next term. The other children were not at such crucial stages of their edu-cation but how could I deal with Alexander and Emily? There was so much to think about, to try to organise. Kirsty and Debbie both urged me to think very carefully about what I was proposing. How would I support us? I knew I had to take drastic action, and couldn't allow my children to be exposed to this situation any longer.

That evening I sat in front of the computer, an idea forming as I visited website after website. Years ago Paul and I had taken the children away for a long weekend to a quaint, unspoilt seaside village in Lincolnshire. I'd been back to the village a few times since with the children, and they loved the beautiful sandy beaches and the freedom they had in this quiet resort. Sutton on Sea was a perfect combination of countryside and seaside, far enough but not too far.

Lincolnshire, like Kent, still had the grammar-school system so Alexander could go to a good school and hopefully the other children would follow suit. That was Alexander accounted for. But what about Emily? She'd achieved fantastic grades in her GCSE mocks and there was no way she would want to leave her school. I certainly didn't think it was in her best interests to do so. And there was also her boyfriend, Shaun, to consider. Things had already been awkward for Emily when his parents asked about her mother, probably wondering how I supported a family of six. She must have wished things were different more than once or twice, that she came from a 'normal' family, whatever that is.

But Emily was all grown-up, as I was constantly reminded – and I thought about the practicalities of her living with her dad and whether this was something I could handle. Paul and I had most certainly had our differences over the years but these had faded in time – the cliché of time being a great healer was true as far as we were concerned. The anger of the divorce had subsided to a level where we were reasonably civil to one another and we'd been able to be there for Victoria when she was ill. He'd worked hard on his demons, and his health was better. He'd also moved out of his parents' place into a very pleasant flat in Chatham. But leaving one of my children behind – how could I even contemplate such a thing? Maybe I was too focused on me? If she was with her father, at the school she had been at for the past six years and still with her boyfriend of over a year, then surely that was best for her . . .

There was a great deal to consider and I needed to do some more research, be sure at least in my mind, then speak to them all. I looked at various estate agents' websites and found that the house prices were considerably less than in Kent, which was a massive plus. Comparatively the prices were amazingly low. I would have to put the house up for sale, find a house up in Lincolnshire and find schools. There was so much to do, but the very first thing was probably the hardest, and that was to talk to the children.

I phoned the Grange and Links Hotel in Sandilands, Lincolnshire, and booked two family rooms for the following week. I told the kids I needed to talk to them all, that we'd be going away the following week for a few days to Sutton on Sea. Emily had a part-time job and exams, so there was no way she could come. Alice was less than enthusiastic but the other children were quite happy to go. Alexander's only concern was his rugby, but when I told him it was a training session this weekend and not a match he was satisfied.

After the four younger ones had gone to bed I told Emily and Alice that I needed to talk to them. I showed them the text message Alexander had received and they were as horrified as I'd been.

'It's one of the reasons I'm seriously thinking of moving us.' In my mind I was certain we'd be going, but I didn't want to present it as a done deal. In fact, I was doing it very much for them.

'We've had great times there. It'll be good for us. A place where nobody knows anything about us, a place we can just live quietly and forget about my work and all that stuff.'

Emily looked at me. 'But –'

'I know – your school, exams, Shaun, everything. Do you think you could live with Dad?' I guess it was two questions really. I was asking her to do it; I was also asking her whether she could handle it. She went silent and I could see her trying to visualise how it would be. I'd leave her to think about it.

Alice was a different matter as there was no question that she was a handful. But she'd really thrown herself into her hairdressing and was enjoying it very much. There are plenty of hairdressers in Lincolnshire, I thought. Plenty of hairdressers everywhere it seemed to me, only outnumbered by estate agents. There was no way I could let her live with Paul – she would run rings round him and she really did need a firm hand. She could see how determined I was and didn't even bother to argue. Besides, she had read the text message and, although neither of them knew anything about the situation with Martin Brookman, they knew I was trying to protect their brothers and sisters.

Emily asked me when I was going to broach the subject with the younger children because I could hardly put the house up for sale without them noticing. She was right. The following day I told the kids that I was thinking about moving to our seaside, which is what we called Sutton. Alexander was reluctant, talking about his friends, his school and his rugby club. The others thought it would be fantastic to live there and to be able to walk on the beach every day. A couple of estate agents came and valued the house and I was pleasantly surprised. I had a friend who ran an estate agents in Strood. I called her and there it was, our house up for sale. I needed a quick sale to get this moving as fast as possible – minimum disruption for the children now that I had made the decision. We all tidied the house like mad, had a handyman come in and do some jobs that had needed doing for ages and made endless trips to the tip, the charity shop and even the local playschool to offload baby toys which seemed to have moved with us last time and stayed unpacked in their boxes in the cellar. Meanwhile I tried to focus Alexander on the positive aspects, like the rugby club and that the grammar school was mixed, and the lovely houses I had seen on the internet, and gradually he came around, albeit very slowly.

The feeling of running away, from the frying pan into the fire, engulfed me. I saw that as the only solution, the only way to escape the pressures of the world I had walked into. So I prepared to run.

I worked several nights in a row, swapping with Trish and Paula, and rearranged the week so I could have four consecutive nights off the following week. As we set off for Sutton on Sea I prayed the weather would be good, the children would love it and we would find the perfect house. If not, I didn't know what else I could do.

Chapter Twenty-Four

*T*he hotel we stayed at was wonderfully old-fashioned and seemed to embody all the quaint idiosyncrasies of an English village. The weather wasn't exactly glorious sunshine; it was after all only April, but the rain held off and in between looking at houses the kids played tennis at the hotel or flew kites on the beach.

We looked at about ten houses over those four days and I found one which I thought was perfect. It had a huge garden for Scooby and the kids, five bedrooms, was about three minutes' walk to the beach and in great condition. Sure, it needed a lick of paint, but didn't every house when you first moved in? The three younger children seemed quite happy about the move by the time we returned home. I would have to make arrangements to visit schools but we could go again to do that once the holidays were over. Alexander was still concerned about the move, such a big change for him to cope with. I remembered how he'd hated the transition from infants school to junior school and now he was faced with moving up to secondary school. People say that children are very adaptable but I don't think they really are. Outwardly, children accept the changes because they have very little or no choice but I think that, just like adults, kids prefer familiarity and shy children find change especially hard to deal with.

Our house gleamed like a new pin and it was a huge trial trying to keep up this new level of cleanliness while life went on. Maureen, the estate agent, tried to give as much notice as possible when she had a potential buyer to show around but sometimes we'd all end up at the last minute whizzing round trying to make the house presentable before yet another family trudged up and down the stairs, peering and inspecting. Finally, we found a buyer; a family who lived on the same road in a much smaller house, and the sale progressed. Once the purchaser's survey had been done I felt confident that we would soon be on our way and out of the mess I had got us into. I had so much to do and asked Trish and Paula to work the odd extra night for me so that I was free to get on with sorting through the house and making another trip to Lincolnshire, this time with Kirsty.

Kirsty and I looked at several houses and finally went to the one I had previously viewed, although I didn't tell her; I wanted to see her reaction. I was relieved when she picked out 'my' house, then confessed that I had actually looked at it before and was going to put an offer in. The cost of the house in Sutton was £40,000 less than I had sold my place for, which was a tremendous help when I was considering how we would now survive financially. We visited the local school, which was lovely, and I made enquiries about enrolling the children there. Unlike in Rochester, the local village primary school had a good reputation and I felt comfortable sending the children there. I knew they would get an education comparable to the standards of the private school I'd been paying for. Alexander would have to take an entrance exam for the grammar school but I didn't see that as a problem – no more school fees, fantastic! Kirsty was reluctant to see me moving so far away but she understood why. The benefits of living in a small rural community were amazing. The freedom the children would have, the beach on their doorstep, the beautiful countryside and, most of all, peace. Sutton was near enough to the market town of Louth and the seaside town of Skegness with their shops and bustle. After a walk around Sutton we drove over to Louth for a look at the school there and the pretty town that surrounded it. According to Kirsty, it all felt like somewhere the Archers would live!

I made the reluctant decision not to send the children back to their school after Easter. I couldn't really see any point as we were moving very soon and had to go to Sutton a few times for Alexander to take his entrance exam, for the other children to have a look around their school and to have another look at the house.

In reality, I was petrified that the kids would be taunted over my business and my past. Four weeks had now passed since Alexander had received the text message and Debbie had admitted the scale of the gossip. Other friends from school had also told me their children had heard various things and asked them questions. I just wanted to protect my children. Of course I would tell them everything, but at a time which I believed was right for us all. The whole story was painful and I wanted to try to explain it to them as gently as I could, answering their questions along the way. It all went back a long way, the debt, my decision to work as an escort, starting an agency – it would be a difficult job to explain it all in a way they could grasp and not frighten them. And Jack's comprehension was obviously very different from Alexander's, given the age difference. Jack wouldn't understand and I certainly didn't want to try to explain any of this to him at his age; it would be unfair.

Emily had finally decided she would live with her dad. She'd have her own room, and getting to and from school would be easy. Of course I found this desperately hard. I'd miss her so much, and so would the other kids, but she had her own life and had to pursue what was best for her. She would be going to university too before long, I tried to tell myself. Paul knew Sutton from our holidays there years before and we had even contemplated moving there years ago, before we were on the road to divorce. I told Paul the same as everybody else; that I was moving for a better quality of life, for the children and for a fresh start. He knew what that meant, as by now I think he'd figured out how I'd been managing to support the family, though he had never brought it up in conversation. He knew that the school fees had been a huge burden to me, that Alexander could go to a grammar school and that I was really happy with the village school. Other than that, Paul didn't really voice much of an opinion. He knew I wasn't particularly interested in his opinions anyway because he had let us all down so badly when we were married.

Having Emily stay with him gave Paul a new lease of life. He seemed so enthusiastic about having her there and I saw glimpses of the man I had fallen in love with so many years ago. I hoped that his parents would want the kids to come and stay with them for weekends to maintain the contact, but I wasn't going to hold my breath for that one.

I sat in the office with a note-pad, scribbling figures and making lists. I talked to myself as I wrote the figures in neat columns. There was a reasonable amount of equity in the house, and with what I had put away and the smaller mortgage we would be fine for a while. Of course, outgoings would be considerably less, now I didn't have to pay the school fees. I wanted to completely disassociate myself from the agency, but how would I do that and what about all the girls who depended on the bookings? How could I just walk away from them? What about Trish and Paula, and the drivers? So many people relied on the agency for their income but what could I do? The problems and responsibilities associated with running an escort agency were huge. I was completely exhausted, not just physically, but mentally too. The late nights, the early mornings, the extra stress of the problems encountered by the girls who worked there, coupled with the preconceived ideas people had about the whole thing, were such an enormous burden.

In the course of the past five years I had lived in a world I'd only read about or seen in movies and on cop shows, never imagining I would somehow be part of it. I thought about the night two years ago when I decided never to work for Holly's agency again. After I had crashed my car through sheer exhaustion, I had driven home knowing that that was it, my life as a prostitute was over. Now I knew that my time running an agency was over. I couldn't live like this any more; the lies, the deceit, the stress of that world was too much to bear. I had seen cocaine, heard conversations that I had no business hearing, and met people whose faces it was best I forgot. What was it about clients in particular that made them so carefree with information as soon as they were in the company of an escort? Maybe in some way they knew that by sharing their secrets they bound you unwillingly into their murky world.

I couldn't have this world knocking on my door any longer; threatening the safe haven I so wanted for my children's lives.

I spoke to Trish, then Paula and told them what I'd decided, that I was going to move away because I just couldn't cope with this life. We would keep everything ticking over until next Monday and I would ring the girls as usual. Apart from anything else, I needed to make sure they paid their fees for the last time. Trish called me an hour or so later with a proposition. They wanted to run the agency themselves, only using the most reliable and trusted girls, reducing the number to about ten. They both needed a job, and this work suited them as they could work from home and the hours suited their lifestyles. The most important thing that Trish pointed out was that they were detached from the intimacy that I had with the girls. The phone number was well known and Trish suggested that she contact BT and make enquiries as to how to take it over. She was utterly serious – they both were. As for the fees, a post-office box number could easily and quickly be arranged. They both urged me to keep things going for a few more weeks while they made the transition, and I agreed but said I only wanted to work one night a week as I had so much to do. We agreed an amount I would be paid for the goodwill of the agency and we had a deal. I felt free. Well, almost.

I felt that a form of closure was coming to us all. Sharon's house was about to complete and her plan to move abroad was neatly tied up. She knew that Colin had been checking up on her almost constantly and was glad she'd told people she was moving to a smaller house locally, and had stuck to her story rigidly. Sharon had not even told the children what was really going on once she realised the lengths Colin was going to. He had followed her on several more occasions, had been into her estate agent asking about the house and, having been told it was under offer, asked whether they had any similar houses. He told them it was a pity the house was under offer because it was perfect – he was sure it was the same house he had looked at months ago when it was up for sale with a previous agent. He remembered the lady saying she was moving away, to which the agent replied she was sure the owner was staying locally, so maybe it wasn't the same house. Colin was so distinct in his appearance that the estate agent remembered him clearly. Sharon had asked the agents if anyone had asked questions about the house or her, and the estate agent had no trouble recalling the creepy little man. As for the kids, Sharon had told them that as soon as the house was sold, they were going on holiday. She couldn't risk Colin finding out, and she had realised by now just how devious he could be.

Finally, completion day arrived for Sharon. Outwardly the house didn't seem any different but she had virtually emptied it of all the possessions which were going with her, and to make life easier the children had been staying with her mum for the past week. Even if Colin had been spying on her 24 hours a day, he would not have realised that the beds had long been stripped of any linen, the cupboards were empty and the freezer defrosted. Always careful, always thinking he was watching, Sharon closed the front door that was no longer hers and drove to her mum's house. She called me as she reached her destination and I phoned Colin's house. He answered the phone and I put the phone down at my end – he was 40 miles away and she was free to go. Sharon picked the kids up and drove to her new life, a fresh start, a second chance. We had said our sad goodbyes and I wondered if I would ever see her again.

A few days later, just as I was getting everything together, Marie rang. She wanted to meet for lunch as she was desperate to show me photos of her new home. We decided to meet at Taj's restaurant for old time's sake. Marie's dream had been a long time coming and, unlike Sharon, she didn't have to hide or sneak away. She'd bought a three-bedroom villa in Nerja, and it was beautiful.

The following weekend she was also going for good, driving down in convoy with two of her sons, only taking what would fit into their cars. Darren was still sulking, still resentful but she prayed that in time they would make their peace and be a family again. Marie looked fantastic, having spent a few long weekends in Spain recently, thanks to the cheap flights from Manston Airport. Gone was the heavy make-up and high heels, and she now had a fresh energy about her, looking forward to her future. Taj joined us for coffee and I told him that Marie was leaving us. He was really pleased for her and said she should be very proud of her achievements, that she deserved happiness and peace at last. How right he was.

Jenny had taken great strides too. She had paid off the loan on her car, had no other debts, and had even invested in an ISA for her future. And she wanted a new future, one that she had never ever thought possible.

With the security of her savings behind her she had decided to apply for a 'proper' job. Jenny wanted to be a classroom assistant, which would obviously fit perfectly with the children and their school holidays. She had applied for a job at her daughter's school and, although she joked about earning less in a week than she could earn in a night, she was looking forward to the normality of her future. Going to bed at a normal time, getting up at a normal time and not feeling like all she wanted to do was sleep forever. Her confidence in her own ability was astounding – the wreck of a girl who had sat before me at that wine bar two years ago had gone and here was a beautiful, confident woman who had so much to give and so much life to live. She had turned her life around and found her self-worth and that there was a decent life out there for her and her children. We sat in my garden watching the kids playing football as she told me of her plans and I was so pleased for her, so happy that some good had come out of all her sacrifice. Her family now had a head start financially and she had plans for their future.

I thought of those women at school to whom people like Jenny were so odious and wondered how much they really understood. Had they ever experienced hardship, seen that people live different lives in very different ways? We all start from different positions, experience different degrees of suffering and trauma. Jenny had started from a so-called 'lower' social class than these women, had only experienced a limited formal education and didn't have a husband and his salary to bring the comfort and security to her life that her critics benefited from. Jenny was worth ten of them and I was proud to call her my friend.

Actually, it wasn't just Sharon, Jenny and Marie whose worlds had changed; all of the girls who had worked at Crystal's had gone through some sort of transformation. Christina had certainly gone through a drastic change in her life. The experience she had suffered at the hands of the transvestite had shocked her to the core. Sometimes one experience, one situation, can do that. The humiliation Christina had felt changed her, and although I would not wish her suffering on anybody, in an absolutely appalling way I think it changed her for the better. Still, no one should ever have to go through such a horrendous experience as hers. But after the attack she stopped believing that she was invincible and saw flaws in herself she had never seen before, or just never acknowledged. She decided to leave her old life behind and take the opportunity to re-train as a physiotherapist, a long hard slog but something she really wanted to achieve. She was prepared to study and endure the three or four years it would take her. I admired her determination, the drive and enthusiasm she had for her new project – that was the old Christina shining through.

Lucy's husband was astounded by the conservatory, the marble fire surround, the wooden flooring throughout the house and the new car. He thought Lucy had worked every hour in overtime and taken a weekend job at a call centre to pay for these things and was really impressed by her efforts. He thought it would take them years to get the house the way they wanted it before they could even think about starting for a family, but they had talked about it and decided that was their next move. I remember asking Lucy if her husband had wanted the house straight before he was prepared to have a family. I had always wondered what her motivation was. The idea that she was prepared to be a prostitute purely for material possessions had always confounded me; feeding the children I understood, but for 'things' I could not comprehend. Lucy said it was along those lines.

It turned out that her husband had had a very deprived childhood, the eighth of a family of ten children, and been determined that when he eventually had kids they would have more than one pair of socks, always have enough to eat and never be cold. He craved a safe happy home, a loving wife, a financially stable environment to bring a child up in. Lucy had worked like a Trojan to make all these things happen; the finance on the car had been paid off, equity in the house vastly improved upon with the addition of the conservatory and the other work she'd had done. She loved him so much she had put herself through a year of prostitution to satisfy his deep-rooted need for security. And now the outgoings were perfectly manageable on one wage, Lucy would stop taking her pill, and hopefully nature would take its course. Lucy's husband would finally be content and the years of pain he had suffered as a child would fade with the new family they would create. I looked at Lucy and finally understood her, finally actually saw *her*. He had no idea of the depth of the love she held for him and I prayed he never would discover what she had to do to get their secure home.

David looked at me in amazement. 'Okay, so let me get this straight. Just like that, just because you have had enough, just because some of the mothers at school are horrible to you, you want to move 300 miles away! Fuck off, Dawn, just fuck off. I don't believe you, there has to be more to it, you don't just bugger off to the other side of the country just like that.'

He was so angry, so hurt, but how could I tell him the real reason, the involvement with Martin, the cocaine that Jenny had been ferrying about, how could I involve him too? David slammed the door as he left, angry, hurt, disbelieving. I couldn't tell him because he would never understand the implications of knowing information about people like Martin Brookman. I would go and he would have to believe it was just because I'd had enough. David was so normal, so unknowing. He wasn't so much naïve, he'd simply never had to deal with the darker side of life because he'd always done everything properly. He'd never been without money, had always been careful and thought in advance, made plans, and provided for his family. I didn't live in that world. I knew too many secrets and had to run away. Running to a safer place would probably cost me David, but if I didn't go I would become even more involved. Martin wouldn't let me escape if I stayed. It's so hard to explain the way people like Martin work, the way their mini-empires envelop you until you either run away or end up one of them.

My intention had been to start a business which supported the children and paid the bills. Well, I achieved that but in the process had also managed to become well known both to the local constabulary and the local criminal fraternity. People make the assumption that girls who work as escorts have a drug problem and are not averse to stealing from their punters. It's a popular myth perpetrated by too much TV. Believe it or not, in all the time I was running the agency, no client ever told me that they had either been robbed by an escort or that a girl had turned up drunk, stoned or high. The Sharons, Maries, Jennys, Isobels and the Lucys of this world do not fall in any of those categories; they are there purely for the electricity bill or the council tax.

I was left looking at the slammed door, listening to David's car start up. I wanted to tell him everything, but there was no point because it wasn't his world. I called David a few days later and asked him to come to Lincolnshire with me and see the house, just to see for himself and tell me what he thought. I explained that it was so much cheaper for me, all the other practical reasons, the financial reasons, the exhaustion I felt through running the agency, the desire to leave that life completely.

Two weeks later on a Friday morning we drove to Sutton on Sea. Of course he loved the house, the beach, the countryside, in fact everything about it, apart from the fact that it was 300 miles away, four hours' drive, nowhere near London or his children. We drove along the coast road, walked on the beach, admired the view, and inside I cried and cried, knowing that it was over for us.

Chapter Twenty-Five

I loaded the black sacks into the back of my car and drove to the charity shop in Rochester High Street. It's amazing how much stuff you accumulate over the years and how little of it you actually decide you really need when it comes to moving.

There were clothes the kids had grown out of, toys they had long since discarded, boxes of pictures painted years ago at playschool, even a cot mobile. And, have you any idea just how many teddy bears six children collect over the years? Memories of happy and sad times, and now all of it was hopefully going to do someone else a good turn via the Barnardo's shop. The cellar had been the worst offender: old trainers, skateboards, coats, a hamster cage with no hamster, but finally we were seeing light at the end of the tunnel and able to concentrate on packing what we were keeping. After the drop-off at Barnardo's, I went on to buy a roll of that bubble wrap that kids love to pop (not adults, of course). I'm not really one for ornaments as such but I did have a few large glass vases which needed careful packing. I had some quotes from various removal companies and the one I'd chosen had already delivered some cardboard boxes.

The kids had been great, sorting through their toys and books and taking an interest in where their unwanted things went. The night before we'd had a discussion about which charity shops we could give things to. The children would have no need for their uniforms so I collected them all together and bagged them up. There was an amazing amount: blazers, boaters, PE kits, tracksuits, summer dresses, winter kilts, and the shirts – there must have been about 30 of them in all. Debbie took a couple of the blazers and some shirts and the rest she took into school for the second-hand uniform shop. I was delighted to hear that she had been accosted by one of the self-righteous mothers as she carried the clothes across the playground. The woman actually took some of the clothes from Debbie there and then, even though she knew they were from my children! Obviously double standards were part of their code.

The packed boxes were neatly stacked up at one end of the lounge. I had written on the boxes what was inside them and which room they were headed for in the new house. I thought it would be less disruptive to have the decorating done as soon as we moved in. I'd had a massive amount of work done at the Rochester house, mainly by two young builders, Gary and Keith, who had agreed to drive up to Sutton with us, help us move in and do as much as was possible over two weeks.

I picked away trying to find the end of the thick brown tape and made up another box, quickly filling it, then repeating the process over again. There were still two weeks to go but I wanted to do as much as possible and be ready. The phone was ringing somewhere in the house and Jack eventually handed it to me. 'It's Charles for you, Mummy.' It was my solicitor. 'Dawn, we have hit rather a large snag. Could you come down and see me, please?' Charles was unwilling to discuss anything over the phone, telling me that it would be better if we talked face to face. With my heart pounding, I grabbed my car keys and told the kids to put their shoes on. Only too pleased at being relieved of their chores, Jack and Victoria came with me to Charles's office in Chatham. The receptionist found paper and pencils for the kids to draw with while Charles ushered me into his office. A second charge had been registered against my house for a huge amount of money – £66,000 to be precise.

After checks with the Land Registry and so many phone calls (it seemed like a million different companies and people were involved) it all went back to 12 years ago, when Paul and I had been in so much negative equity we had decided to hand back the keys to the little terraced house we had been living in. Having never heard any more about it coupled with the fact that years had passed, I had forgotten all about it and I'm sure Paul had too. It emerged that the debt had been sold from the original mortgage company to another company, and so it had gone on having been sold several more times for a paltry amount until now, when a regular check at the Land Registry had alerted the company who now owned the debt that the house was about to be sold. They had registered the charge, which had to be discharged at the time of completion to allow the sale to proceed. All that equity would be gone and I would be absolutely broke. What was I going to do? Charles explained that he had to satisfy the charge the mortgage company had over the house, then pay any other charges before he could release the residue of any funds to me and, as it stood, there would be nothing. I understood what he was saying and it registered somewhere, but what about all my plans for a fresh start, another chance? Thanking Charles for his time, I collected the kids and drove home, biting my lip to stop the tears. I was so upset, too tired to think straight and decided to fight the fight tomorrow.

In the morning Kirsty came over and looked after the kids while I shut myself in the office and called Stephen, the managing director of the company that was about to smash my future. I told him what his company was doing to me. He had no personal knowledge of the situation but said he would do some research and call me back after 2.00 pm. Until then I kept my mind off it by packing the rest of the toys, clothes and bedding, washing out cupboards, cleaning windows, dusting away cobwebs and wiping down shelves. Kirsty and I made lunch for all the kids and ate outside as it was such a lovely day, but I felt so anxious and Kirsty helpless. At 2.20 pm Stephen called me back, thoroughly researched. He sounded genuinely sorry as I told him that the first I'd heard of this was the call from my solicitor the previous day. He agreed that there was a ridiculous amount of interest and said he'd see what could be done.

The rest of the day passed so painfully slowly. Kirsty and I went through my kitchen drawers, marvelling at the rubbish we found, a shell from the beach, pebbles with faces painted on them, once treasured possessions of my children that were now long-forgotten mementoes, discarded and meaningless. I threw away drinks bottles without lids, lunchboxes without catches, containers I had washed out and saved. I found the corkscrew we had lost, Alexander's Sports Captain badge, a few two-pound coins and a penny. I might need them now. Kirsty stayed for supper and we ate fish and chips from their paper in the garden.

'Ah well. You can always go back on the game,' she joked.

'Yeah, thanks, love. I just might do that,' I smiled, knowing that I never would.

Stephen called back the following day. Victoria came and found me in Alexander's room, stripping his bed for the washing. She gave me the phone and said it was a nice man called Stephen and she'd been telling him all about how she played rugby. Stephen had indeed had a long chat with Victoria and thought she was highly amusing. He had kids himself and realised that, after all this time, it must be a huge blow and I'd been left to pay for a problem that was not solely my responsibility. He said it was just the luck of the draw. Sometimes companies like his got lucky and caught up with people like me who had accrued debts from years ago but often they slipped through the net. 'Forget the £66,000 figure. Make me an offer.' He told me the actual amount of negative equity was just under £28,000 – the balance was interest and costs. I offered him £5,000, he asked for £15,000 and we settled on £9,000.

I called Charles and told him what I had done and he was astounded at the figure I'd managed to negotiate. Stephen had agreed to fax a letter to Charles that afternoon, write to me to confirm the figure and then the sale of the house could proceed. I called Maureen, the estate agent, and confirmed the sale was going ahead. The relief was tangible – in fact you could have picked up bucketfuls of the stuff.

I was annoyed that this had cost me £9,000 but it was dealt with and we could move on. You can't get away with anything these days and it's so much simpler not to have to try. There really are ways and means to deal with problems like debt management. Okay, hindsight is a wonderful thing and we really only learn once we have experienced something at first hand. I ran away from an obligation and paid for it many times over in stress and anxiety and eventually with money.

A week to go, and we were just about ready. I still had to do last-minute things like defrost the fridge and disconnect the washing machine, but everything else was packed and ready to go. Each day that passed brought more excitement for the kids and more anxiety for me. I kept asking myself if I was doing the right thing, if this was really the answer. Sharon was ecstatically happy in her new life so why shouldn't I be? I pushed all the questions, all the worries to one side and concentrated on the practical and logistical problems ahead.

I'd taken Scooby up to Lincolnshire two weeks before when Alexander had sat the entrance exam for his new school. I thought he would be better off in kennels where they had a regular routine instead of all the upheaval of the move. Once we had moved in and the bulk of the work was done I could bring him home. We were eating very peculiar food, made up of whatever was left in the freezer. I could see our last few meals in Rochester all being takeaways. The children had said their goodbyes to friends; we had that many farewells it felt like we were moving to Australia, not a few hours up the motorway. I had arranged for us all to stay at Paul's flat on our last night in Rochester because it made life easier for the removal men and for Gary and Keith who were helping with the last few things like taking the beds down and dealing with the washing machine.

My office was long packed up; Trish and Paula were running the agency and only occasionally called me with a problem. We had decided to tell the girls that we were scaling things down due to lack of business and therefore would be letting some of them go. To the other girls, the more reliable ones that between us we had chosen to stay on, I explained that although I would still be around I now had other commitments so would be less involved, and Trish or Paula would take their weekly details. I was so pleased not to be involved in the day-to-day running but inevitably there were still problems now and again which needed attention.

Despite my own working past, my very personal approach and my efforts to keep their working lives secret for them, the image I seemed to have with these girls was of some madam who fronted an agency for some big gangland boss. It was something they perhaps found helpful with clients and maybe they ended up believing it themselves. No one is going to bounce a cheque or walk out without paying when they think you work for a powerful, probably violent organisation. It was hilarious really; the questions the girls asked Trish and Paula about me and who I *really* worked for. Some of them probably bought into the rumours of a business connection with Martin Brookman! I guess that's the preconceived idea so many people hold about escort agencies and brothels – all smoke and mirrors, big money and muscle. In most cases, it simply isn't true.

I had dropped the kids at Paul's flat with a takeaway and a DVD. There was no way they would go to sleep early tonight; there was far too much excitement buzzing through them. I came back to the house in Rochester one last time. Virtually everything had gone, loaded up that day by the removal men, who would come back in the morning for the few last items, the kids' bikes and my lovely Silver Cross carriage pram that for no fathomable reason I was taking with us. It was huge, something an Edwardian nanny would push around the park, but my last four babies had been walked for miles in it and it was coming to Lincolnshire too. Perhaps one day, many years in the future, I would have a grandchild in need of a pram. I remembered to do the sensible things like locate the stop-cock and turn the water off at the mains. I took the meter readings then flicked the switch on the fuse box – another tedious job ticked off.

I stood in what had been my bedroom and looked out of the window at the street below. It was nearly Midsummer's Day, so still very light. For the last time I saw neighbours coming home from work, carrying shopping, walking their dogs. Satisfied that everything was spotless, I walked down to what had been Jack's room and opened the door wide. With such a mix of emotions I walked from room to room, checking for the last time that we hadn't left anything behind, that everything was clean and tidy, that the instructions for the alarm had been left for the new owners. Everything that should be was locked and bolted; all the windows were shut tight. I opened all the internal doors to let the air circulate as it was so warm.

I had been so proud of this house when we had first moved here and begun to renovate and decorate. I touched my beautiful fireplace and thought about all the effort that had gone into making it as gorgeous as it now was. I thought about the birthday parties, the friends sitting around our massive table, having lunch or dinner. Sharon and I dancing on the table to Shania Twain, the kids rolling around on the floor laughing. It was only a house and what mattered were the memories, and those I would be taking with me. The new house would be far away from the agency and what it brought with it, people like Martin Brookman and his cronies. Away from gossip and rumours, malicious, judgemental people who didn't stop to consider just how much hurt they were causing. I locked the front door behind me for the very last time, climbed into my car and drove away to Paul's flat and the first part of the journey back to the normal world had begun. It was a journey that would take time, a great deal of time, because people have long memories.

Chapter Twenty-Six

'About four hours', I told the kids, 'it'll take about four hours. You've done it loads of times before now, so stop asking and let's get going.'

We were at the petrol garage next to Paul's flat. The car was piled up with quilts, pillows, snacks, drinks, Game Boys, Walkmans, clothes, magazines – all the usual things that kids insist on taking to fight the boredom on tedious journeys. Paul checked the tyres for me, the oil and the water. I filled up with petrol, bought a bag of mints and a bottle of water, drove out of the Medway towns and pointed the car towards the M2. We queued to go through the Dartford Tunnel, singing along to some CD the kids had finally all agreed on.

I was scared, praying silently that I was making the right decision, doing the right thing. Too late now, no going back; the deal was done. Around the M25, up the M11 and only a couple of stops for the loo, Jack doing his customary peeing in a bottle when he decided he was desperate and there was no hard shoulder to pull over on. You know you are in Lincolnshire because the ground is so flat.

Finally we drove into South Road and up the driveway of number ten. Gary and Keith had arrived and had rung me to say they'd collected the keys. The removal men had been and gone a couple of hours ago, unloading everything into the huge double garage to one side of the front garden. There was no point in doing anything much today other than putting a few beds up and digging out the linen. After the initial excitement which had seen the kids running up and down the stairs, exploring the house and garden, I had gone off in search of fish and chips and drinks. We had a stroll down to the beach, feeling like holidaymakers but harbouring the excitement of staying for that bit longer than everyone else.

The following day a skip arrived and the really hard work began. We pulled up old carpets, ripped out an old fireplace, took down old curtains, cleaned, scrubbed, unpacked where possible and fell into bed absolutely exhausted at midnight. Every part of me ached. The younger children started school on Monday morning. I was anxious for them to do this as soon as possible, to make some friends before the summer holidays and hopefully settle in quickly. They loved the fact that they could walk to school or ride their bikes and be there in five minutes. I often rode with them or met them afterwards on my bike. They only had four weeks until they broke up for the summer holidays and

251

I knew they would be spending most of their time on the beach. With the huge hurdle of the new school out of the way, I felt we were really beginning to settle in. Gary, Keith, Alice and I worked so hard every day of those two weeks, painting, sanding, unpacking and cleaning until finally the house was really beginning to look like a home.

Alice would be starting her new school in September too, in a last-ditch attempt to give school a final try. It was a much-needed chance, I thought, for her to make some new friends after the disastrous departure from her last school. Absolutely exhausted, Gary and Keith left us after transforming the house into a new home and as I watched them drive away I felt so lonely, so absolutely alone, so isolated and scared. They had been my last connection to all that was familiar and now they were gone and this was reality. Better get used to this, I said to myself.

The summer holidays were blissful. Kirsty and Maggie came up with their kids for a few days, and the time was spent gossiping and catching up, having picnics on the beach and all the other typical English seaside activities. Sarah came to stay with her daughters and two grandchildren and again we had a peaceful relaxing few days. The weather was wonderful; the kids were so happy; all the ingredients for a perfect existence.

Life went from the ridiculous to the sublime in the space of a few months. It seemed like one moment I had been running an escort agency, involved with drug dealers and all manner of sexual deviants; and the next, I was pleased that the tomatoes I had planted were growing so well and making chutney and jam, helping out with the reading at school. Debbie's kids came to stay and they loved the freedom, the open space, the peace. We went up to East Yorkshire to stay with friends, and only had about an hour and a half to drive instead of the usual seven hours. The village school was excellent; the children thrived and loved every minute of it. They were all so happy and so far away from intrusion into their lives, so secure and safe.

I missed David a great deal but there was no way it would have been possible for him to be here with me. His work was in London, his children in Kent; I knew it was no use while 300 miles separated us but I ached for him every second of every day. The agony I felt watching him drive away after the first weekend he spent with us in Sutton tore me to pieces. He called me as soon as he arrived safely back at his house; tired, sad and confused. We both knew that there was no way we could have a relationship living this far apart. So while my heart cried for me, my head smiled for the children.

I did see Sharon again when she came to stay with us for a few days. She'd managed to move on, was happy and had left everything about her former life behind her. She hardly wore any make-up, and looked tanned and fresh. I think it was relief, peace of mind and the security of knowing that she had made it through the lies, deceit, exhaustion and sheer madness of what had become her life. She looked softer and was happy, at long, long last.

We talked about Colin, about the mess she'd been in with him, how she'd managed to escape from it all without the children or any of her other family or friends ever knowing about her escorting life or the existence of a Colin. He had called the agency and told Paula he'd been trying to find her. And when Trish took his call one night, she told him he wasn't the only one looking for Sharon, that she owed the agency loads of money and they'd be very grateful to have any information; in turn they'd tell him everything we knew. Colin called another evening and said a neighbour had heard Sharon had gone back to Newcastle where she was originally from, and another had said Scotland. So Colin unwittingly kept us informed and in turn Trish could warn Sharon, just in case. By now he'd been told there were so many people looking for Sharon and that he was so far down the pecking order he might as well whistle. Sharon always had to live with what she had done to Colin, but hopefully she learned from her experiences.

For years my life had been a rollercoaster. Sometimes I'd felt as though I was hanging upside down, but now the ride had come to a complete standstill, and I was the right way up. I'd met people who had had a profound effect on my life, and made some wonderful friendships, had an insight into bizarre relationships and felt completely humbled by the achievements of the girls who had come to work with me, a few of whom had become solid friends. For now at least, the children and I were happy and content. This life would do for the time being. I would look for a job. I had thought about catering for dinner parties and private functions. It was just a whim but I might as well start with something I was good at, and cooking was one thing I love to do. Or I could go back to secretarial work. Lots of ideas muddled through my head, lots of possibilities but for now it didn't really matter. So long as we had enough to get by, enough to manage on, I was happy.

I know I've been judged and there's nothing I can do about that. My kids have a stable and happy life and that's exactly what I wanted. I didn't achieve my goal the conventional way but I really felt I had no choice. Of course I've made mistakes, but haven't we all? And it's true that some came back to haunt me. The life I was leading did scare me at times but I'm in a very different place now.

I remember sitting on the beach with Sharon one day. She turned and said to me, 'You know, you could write a book about what's happened to you.'

'No one would believe me,' I said, and I turned to watch the waves lapping on the sand.

Epilogue

*I*n 2005 my memoir *Call Me Elizabeth* was published and I was amazed at how well it was received. The media was hugely interested and I was asked to talk about the book on many radio shows, was interviewed on TV and was featured in newspapers and magazines.

I received hundreds of emails, some of which were criticisms, but most of which were messages of support. So many people said they understood my reasons for becoming an escort and felt they might have done the same under those circumstances.

People have been very forthright with their views, both at the time and now, and I often find that women I would never have expected to support me did just that. Even though time, and the writing of the memoir, had laid to rest some of my own issues with my past, it still felt good, still helpful somehow to receive positive feedback. Many working women told me how they identified with the problems I had while trying to provide for my family as a single parent, and were heartened by the fact that they were not alone. The one thing that saddened me was the number of women who emailed saying that they were considering becoming an escort. I would hate anyone to go through what I did, and I tried to direct these women to debt conciliation services or other appropriate agencies, advising them to do anything but become an escort.

My children were aged between nine and 19 at the time of publication. The two eldest knew about my past and understood that I was writing a book about a very sensitive time of my life, and also that there would be a certain amount of media interest. The middle two also knew about the book and when it was being published. The youngest two knew that Mummy had written a book about when she used to work in the night-time. When the book was published some of my friends took the kids on holiday for two weeks to Lanzarote so that they were away while the book was receiving media attention.

Obviously I wanted publicity in the hope that my story would help others, but also because I wanted the book to sell. But at the same time, I did not want the children to be ostracised or exposed to name-calling. Fortunately, their friends were not interested and the kids were unaffected. I felt very uncomfortable for the first few months after publication when I was at school picking up the kids, but eventually I decided I was not going to allow anyone's judgement to affect me.

When the first book was published we were still living in Lincolnshire. Victoria was very unwell at the time and we needed to travel to London every three weeks for hospital appointments. The journeys were exhausting and expensive, so I made the decision to move us to Folkestone. It was much closer to London and was still by the sea where we rented a house. During this time, I started to see David again.

I left the end of *Call Me Elizabeth* open for a sequel as there seemed to be two distinct halves to my story: first, becoming an escort, and second, deciding to start my own agency. I had so many emails from people asking me what had happened next, that I started to write *Call Me Madam*.

With no guarantee that my second book would be published, and income from *Call Me Elizabeth* slowing down, I found myself with money problems once more – without a stable job and with the children to look after. On top of this, David and I broke up again after a number of fights, many of them about money.

I was at a very low point in my life and found myself facing a county court hearing for owing money to my landlord. Without David to support me through the situation I felt incredibly lonely and powerless. There seemed to be no way out and, with both money and relationship problems, I became very depressed. I even considered going back to escorting again – everything seemed to be going wrong at once. In blind desperation, I phoned the police and falsely claimed the house had been broken into and I had been sexually assaulted in the stupid hope I could buy some time to pay them back. It was a stupid, terrible thing to do and I can't justify it on any rational grounds. In the course of the police investigation, the truth came out and I was taken to court, where I pleaded guilty to wasting police time. I received a suspended jail sentence and was ordered to pay compensation.

We all have to accept responsibility for our actions and I know that, however much I would like to, and however sorry I am, I can't turn the clock back on what I did. Since that terrible time I have started to make the most of opportunities I have and have pieced my life back together.

In 2007 we took the decision as a family to move to Spain. We have some good friends here and the move has been very positive for all of us. The children are in Spanish schools and enjoying the sunshine. I'm backwards and forwards to England for various reasons and haven't yet had time to miss the cold and rain.

As *Call Me Madam* is about to go to press, I am busy writing a novel and, most importantly, the kids are happy and healthy. Life is pretty much back to normal, and I spend my days doing what most mums do – fitting in work with the very active lives of my children. I'm a taxi service, cook, laundress, social secretary, etc. Luckily I can fit my writing and research around the children, as I am still very privileged to be able to work from home.

My first two books were so much hard work and research, but were a testament to the wonderful people I encountered. A huge proportion of society is made up of incredibly vulnerable people who have far too often suffered abuse and neglect of one form or another.

My interests now are in prison reform, helping to find a way to break the cycle of abuse, neglect, vulnerability, crime, addiction and other dire aspects of our society. So many people suffer so much and survive, but only just, and I hope that through voluntary work and writing I can help give something back in some tiny way.

If I knew then what I know now, I probably would have done things differently – but I guess that's the benefit of hindsight. I can only say that I'm human and I made mistakes. Although I am no longer associated with the escort business, I still think about the women I worked with – brave, hardworking women who just wanted the best for their children.

My kids are happy, which is the most important thing in the world to me. And as for my love life, David and I got back together and have sorted out our differences and have a great relationship once more and my career as a writer is firmly on track. All I can say is that in the end, everything has worked out for the best.

Forget You Had a Daughter
Doing Time in the Bangkok Hilton – Sandra Gregory's Story

Sandra Gregory with Michael Tierney

Forget You Had a Daughter is the bestselling autobiography of Sandra Gregory, who was arrested for smuggling heroin out of Thailand. Sandra was living and working in Bangkok when she fell ill, lost her jobs and ran out of money. Desperate to get home, she accepted a junkie's offer to smuggle his personal heroin supply. It took her over seven years to get home. She graphically tells of being sentenced to death (which was commuted to 25 years), the horrific conditions in Lard Yao prison, dubbed the 'Bangkok Hilton', and of being shunted around the British prison system after her transfer.

Following a pardon from the King of Thailand in 2000, she has raised money for a hospice in Lard Yao, given talks in schools about her experiences and is about to commence study at Oxford University.

This is the unforgettable story of a good woman who made a mistake that changed the rest of her life.

VISION PAPERBACKS
Memoir
978-1-905132-27-1
£6.99

Confessions of a Showman
My Life in the Circus

Gerry Cottle with Helen Batten

The sensational memoir of Gerry Cottle, the greatest ever circus boss.

Gerry, a stockbroker's son, ran away to join the circus when he was just 15. Within a few years he had married into Britain's oldest circus dynasty and started his very own circus.

Living on his wits and the advice of old-timers he created the largest circus in the world, hiring the best acts like clown Charles Caroli and Captain Universe the cannonball man. He invented the Circus on Ice and learnt how to put his head inside a crocodile's mouth, before his growing cocaine addiction led to his arrest and bankruptcy.

Always the 'comeback king', Gerry squared up to animal rights protestors and made millions with the first ever non-animal circus, the Moscow and Chinese State circuses, and the Circus of Horrors.

Packed with hilarious stories of circus acts gone wrong, girls chased and family feuds, this no-holds-barred memoir is the extraordinary life story of the ultimate showman.

VISION PAPERBACKS
Memoir
978-1-905745-16-6
£6.99

For a House Made of Stone
Gina's Story

Gina French with Andrew Crofts

The extraordinary true story of a young woman from the Philippines who, aged 27, stood trial in the UK for the murder of her husband.

All Gina wanted was to support her family and protect them from the elements by building them a house made of stone. Her quest took many turns – from the fleshpots of Manila to the jet-set worlds of New York and Brunei – until she fell in love with a British man. She married him and together they had a son.

She soon realised that she was married to an abusive bully, but she agreed to move to England to salvage their relationship. Driven close to madness by her husband's violence, Gina stabbed him. Suddenly she was facing a murder charge in a foreign land where she understood little of what was going on.

For a House Made of Stone is Gina's uniquely inspiring story of love, loss, survival and hope.

VISION PAPERBACKS
Memoir
978-1-904132-80-6,
£10.99